HEBREWS 11

Wisdom Commentary Series: Hebrews 11

Author: Stephen Davey
Editor: Jarl K. Waggoner
Body Layout: Kristin Preston
Cover Layout: Kent Perigo
Photo of Stephen: Tierney Riggs Braddock, (https://www.tierneyriggsphotography.com/)
ISBN 978-1-944189-37-2
© 2020 Stephen Davey. All rights reserved.

Unless otherwise noted, all Scripture quotations are from the New American Standard Bible® (NASB),

© 1960, 1962, 1963, 1968, 1971, 1972, 1973, 1975, 1977, 1995 by the Lockman Foundation. Used by permission. www.Lockman.org

Scripture quotations marked NIV are taken from The Holy Bible, New International Version® NIV®

Copyright © 1973, 1978, 1984, 2011 by Biblica, Inc.™ Used by permission. All rights reserved worldwide.

Scripture quotations marked KJV are from the King James Version of the Bible.

Published by Charity House Publishers

Charity House Publishers, Inc.
2703 Jones Franklin Road
Suite 105
Cary, NC 27518
USA
www.wisdomonline.org

*With deepest appreciation for
the faithful ministry of
~ the elders ~
who courageously, biblically and humbly lead,
on behalf of Jesus Christ and for His glory,
Colonial Baptist Church.*

CONTENTS

1. The Drumbeat of Faith 7
   Hebrews 11:1–2

2. The Ultimate, Original Hero 17
   Hebrews 11:3

3. Beyond the Cherubim 29
   Hebrews 11:4

4. The First to Vanish 41
   Hebrews 11:5–6

5. Fleeing the City of Destruction 53
   Hebrews 11:7

6. Waiting on the Promises of God 75
   Hebrews 11:8–22

7. From Riches to Rags 87
   Hebrews 11:23–28

8. Faith from the Unlikely 99
   Hebrews 11:29–31

9. An Ancient Memorial 109
   Hebrews 11:32–35a

10. Living in the Shadows 123
    Hebrews 11:35b–40

Endnotes 135

Scripture Index 143

¹*Now faith is the assurance of things hoped for, the conviction of things not seen.* ²*For by it the men of old gained approval.*

–Hebrews 11:1–2

CHAPTER ONE

THE DRUMBEAT OF FAITH

Hebrews 11:1-2

When I was a young boy and school was out for the summer, my mother used to let my brothers and me spend afternoons in one of our favorite downtown places. It was a large, white stone building called The Main Norfolk Library. I can still smell the aroma that greeted me as I entered that building, which housed tens of thousands of volumes waiting to be discovered. I usually left the library with an armload of biographies of people who would become my heroes: men like Davy Crocket, Lewis and Clark, George Washington Carver, and Louis Pasteur.

One biography worth reading was that of Louis Pasteur (1822-95), who invented a process that killed pathogenic bacteria by the application of heat, thus preventing diseases caused by spoiled milk. The process, later named after him, would be called "pasteurization."[1]

He also developed the first vaccine for rabies.[2] Axel M. F. Munthe, a medical doctor associated with Pasteur, recounts an interesting episode that took place when Pasteur was in the laboratory attempting to create the vaccine. Munthe tells us: "Pasteur himself was absolutely fearless. I once saw him, with the glass tube held between his lips, secure a few drops of the deadly saliva from the mouth of a rabid bull-dog, held on the table by two assistants, their hands protected by leather gloves."[3] As Pasteur collected the sample he needed, his face was inches from the foaming mouth of the rabid dog. He deserves hero status.

Another biography I devoured as a young boy was that of George Washington Carver, a freed slave who in the early 1900s discovered invaluable methods of crop development. Among his amazing discoveries, he found three hundred different ways to use peanuts, including his tastiest invention of all—peanut butter.[4] He certainly qualifies for hero status. Between pasteurized milk and peanut butter, you have the basic necessities of life!

Has it ever occurred to you that God is deeply interested in retelling the lives of men and women throughout history? We tend to learn best when truth is brought to life. For this reason, among others, God brings truth onstage for us in Scripture through the biographies of people, both good and bad, virtuous and wicked, spiritual and sensual, sacrificial and self-absorbed. Indeed, the majority of the Bible is biographical, narrating the histories of men and women, kings and nations, pioneers and prophets.

G. Campbell Morgan, a man considered to be the prince of expositors in both Great Britain and America in the 1900s, once wrote, "Experience is a hard teacher and there are those who never learn."[5] Maybe we never learn because we don't read enough biographies.

It is no surprise, then, to read the following statements God made through His apostles about people in the past:

- Paul wrote: "For whatever was written in earlier times was written for our instruction, so that through perseverance and the encouragement of the Scriptures we might have hope" (Romans 15:4).

- Referring to Israel's history, Paul also made this comment: "Now these things happened to them as an example, and they were written for our instruction" (1 Corinthians 10:11).

- According to the author of Hebrews, we must become "imitators of those who through faith and patience inherited the promises" (Hebrews 6:12). Since it is impossible to imitate someone you don't know, God allows us to get to know them through biblical biography.

God has given us the biographies of people—and even nations—to establish our hope and teach us how to live and walk by faith.

THE DRUMBEAT OF FAITH

One of the most remarkable biographic sections of the Bible is found in the epistle to the Hebrews, written to Jewish Christians surrounded by trouble and persecution. In the eleventh chapter, God selects a dozen biographies of faithful pioneers. The background of this selection appears at the end of chapter 10, where the author exhorts: "Do not throw away your confidence" (verse 35). In other words, "Don't give up, no matter how bad it looks and how difficult it gets. Remember these servants of God who walked by faith."

In chapter 12, the writer of Hebrews encourages suffering readers: "Therefore, since we have so great a cloud of witnesses surrounding us . . . let us run with endurance the race that is set before us" (verse 1). Or we could paraphrase it this way: "Since you've now discovered that you are surrounded by this great cloud of witnesses—all these testimonies of the saints of old—keep pressing on, running the race set before you."

God exhorts us, not only to live by faith, but also to run by faith. And Hebrews 11 shows us how.

What appears to be a parenthesis between chapters 10 and 12 serves to reveal the biographies of believers who, though imperfect, saw the invisible and pursued the impossible. They walked to the drumbeat of faith.

THE DEFINITION OF FAITH

Before we are introduced to these individual heroes of faith, the author writes: **Now faith is the assurance of things hoped for, the conviction of things not seen** (Hebrews 11:1).

Upon reading this verse, one can easily understand why Bible students in general immediately conclude that this is a *definition* of biblical faith. We assume that faith *is* assurance and conviction about things we're hoping for but cannot yet see. We're left wondering, *How do I get that kind of assurance? How do I develop that kind of conviction?*

There are several ways we can define something. First, a given thing can be defined *objectively*; that is, based on what it *looks* like. Second, it can be defined *subjectively*, explaining what it *feels* like. And third, something can be defined *functionally*, or in light of what it *acts* like.

Suppose I place a bicycle in front of you. If I were to define it objectively, I would say, "The word *bicycle* is a compound word made up of two words: *bi*, for *two*, and *cycle*, for *wheels*. The tires are made of rubber and are mounted on wheels, which have spokes for reinforcement and are attached to a metal frame. On top of the frame is a seat upon which you sit. There are handlebars on the front end, so you can steer the bicycle in the direction you desire, and to which you can hold as you ride through town." In this case, I would be describing the object, thus providing an objective definition.

I could also choose to explain, "If you will sit on this seat and ride off, you will experience a wonderful sensation. You'll have a front row seat to the beauty of your surroundings—the sunlight directly in your face, and the wind whipping through your hair (or what's left of it). There's nothing quite like the thrill of riding a bicycle." This would be the subjective definition of *bicycle*—what it means to experience it.

But I could also describe how the bicycle operates: "You sit on the seat, put one foot on the pedal and then push ahead. Immediately after, place your other foot on the other pedal, and balance yourself as you begin to pump the pedals. This way, you'll be able to ride along." In this instance, I would be defining bicycle functionally—how it operates.

In Hebrews 11, the author offers a *functional* description of faith, not a factual definition.[6] He is describing what faith *does*. Throughout the entire chapter, the Spirit of God shows us how to live by faith by means of practical demonstrations, not theoretical definitions—we're shown *how* to ride the bicycle of faith.

Three principles emerge from the opening remarks in Hebrews 11.

PRINCIPLES OF FAITH

Faith and Hope

Now faith is the assurance of things hoped for.
(Hebrews 11:1*a*)

The first principle is that *faith continually provides a foundation for our hope*. It is **the assurance of things hoped for**. Other translations read: "Now faith is confidence in what we hope for" (NIV); and, "faith is the substance of things hoped for" (KJV). The words **assurance**, *confidence*, and *substance* all convey the underlying meaning of the original Greek term *hupostasis*. It literally refers to that which "stands under" as support. Thus, this assurance, confidence, or substance refers to the *foundation* upon which our hope stands.[7]

And for what do we hope?

- Christ's return for His church
- Our future glorified bodies
- A reunion of all the departed believers in heaven
- The coming of the literal earthly kingdom, when Christ will reign on earth and we will reign with Him
- Our future dwelling in the Father's house as it permanently descends to a newly created earth

Our faith does not make these things true; it simply embraces the truth.[8] And we know these things to be true by means of our faith in the inspired words of God, which continually build a foundation upon which we stand.

The truth is, even the secular world is uneasy in its growing conviction that there is more out there beyond the present life. I was in a pharmacy some time ago, being helped by a teenage girl at the cash register. I said to her, "I hope you're having a good day."

"Well, my foot is bothering me," she replied, explaining that she had been hurt in a soccer game, ruining her hopes of being a dancer.

I stated, "You know God has a reason for everything."

She said, "I know. It's given me time to focus on my religion. You see, I'm a pagan."

"I know some people like that," I continued. "Tell me what it means to you." The girl told me she was studying earth worship and witchcraft. I asked: "What do you plan to do?"

She answered, "I want to start my own coven one day." When I asked what she wanted to do after that, she replied, "I want to start my own earth church." I thought it was interesting she still wanted to go to church.

"Then what are you going to do after that?" I asked.

She said, "I don't know . . . maybe become a teacher."

Looking at her, I said, "What are you going to do one minute after you die?"

She twisted her hands together, smiled, and then said, "I don't know. I hope the divine will be good to me."

I was intrigued by her response, so I asked: "So you believe in God after all?"

She answered, "Well, no, not like that, you know. I mean . . . whatever."

At that point in the conversation, I noticed another customer was ready to check out, so I left, but not before asking her to think about those questions a little more. I pray she will.

This short conversation exposed how rickety her foundation was. It was unable to withstand the test of simple questions. She knew there was something more "out there," but her hopes were built on a flawed foundation that gave her no real, consistent hope.

The biblical faith, on the other hand, continually provides a solid foundation for all our hopes. Our faith is not wistful longing, simply hoping that something will come to pass someday.[9] In this regard, it would be true to assert that biblical faith is not a feeling, but it would also be true to state that faith *affects* our feelings. The growing foundation for our hope causes us to long for the redemption of our bodies (Romans 8:23), urgently deliver the gospel to the lost (2 Corinthians 5:20), love and humbly serve fellow believers (Colossians 3:12-25), and anticipate the return of Christ (1 Thessalonians 1:10).

Although faith is not a feeling—it is our foundation—it impacts our feelings greatly.

If your friend told you he had just deposited a million dollars in your bank account, how would you feel? What kind of emotions would you experience as you drove over to check out your new bank balance? The way you drove to the bank and how you felt while driving there would be determined by how much faith you had in the promise of your friend. If you really trusted him, you would maintain the speed limit; you might wait until tomorrow afternoon to stop by the bank; you might even mail out some checks without ever going to the bank at all! Your faith in the promise of your friend would make all the difference.

Our faith and resultant feelings are really nothing more than our confidence in the promises of God.

Faith and Conviction

Now faith is . . . the conviction of things not seen. (Hebrews 11:1*b*)

The second principle is that *faith produces a conviction that invisible things exist.* The King James Version reads "faith is . . . the evidence of things not seen."

The Greek word translated conviction or *evidence* appears only here in the entire New Testament. It refers to proof.[10] Aristotle employed it to refer to a convincing argument.[11] Our faith is the convincing argument for, or proof of, an invisible world.

The inspired author does not state that our faith *proves* invisible things exist; he writes that our faith is the proof invisible things exist. Our faith is enough, for it is anchored to the written Word of the living Lord.

What are these invisible things of which we have become convinced?

- The cross of Christ is sufficient to pay the penalty for our sins.
- Jesus Christ was raised from the dead and sits at the right hand of the Father.
- The risen Savior intercedes continually on our behalf.
- The Word of God we proclaim is never void or fruitless.
- The ministry of the Holy Spirit is a reality.
- Ongoing spiritual attacks are attempts to discourage, defeat, and discredit us.
- Demons and angels actually exist.

I wear glasses, not because I want to, but because I need to. They correct the weaknesses in my eyes brought on by age. A fisherman can buy special sunglasses that remove much of the glare so that he can spot fish below the surface of the water (evidently that's what I've needed). A soldier can use night vision goggles to track enemy movements in the dark.

Faith functions in a very similar way for the benefit of the believer. Eyesight proves the reality of the physical world; faith proves the reality of the spiritual world.

- Like corrective lenses, faith compensates for our spiritual weaknesses.
- Like a pair of fisherman's sunglasses, faith helps us to see beyond the glare around us and focus on our mission as "fishers of men."
- Like night vision goggles, faith allows us to spot our enemy, that old serpent who puts a trap in our path. Faith helps us to see in the dark.[12]

God often brings us to a place where we cannot depend on our own senses but only on the Spirit. The maturing Christian trusts in the Spirit more than he does his senses. He understands that while his eyes give him physical sight, it is his faith that gives him insight into a spiritual world that is real.[13]

We find a real-life demonstration of this principle in 2 Kings 6. The Arameans were plotting to capture the prophet Elisha and kill him. The king sent a great army during the night to surround the city where Elisha was staying. The biblical record informs us that the next morning Elisha's assistant got up early, went outside, and saw that "an army with horses and chariots was circling the city." So he ran back inside, woke Elisha up, and said, "Alas, my master! What shall we do?" (2 Kings 6:15). Elisha then made this rather amazing statement to his associate: "Do not fear, for those who are with us are more than those who are with them" (verse 16).

I can just hear the assistant saying, "Elisha, you might be good at prophesying, but you're lousy at math. Where are all those who are with us? If my math serves me right, there's one of you and one of me, which makes two of us, but surrounding us is an army of at least a thousand trained warriors, with state-of-the-art military equipment (horses and chariots). You have your walking stick, and I guess I can throw some rocks! What are we going to do?" So Elisha prayed that the Lord would open the servant's eyes that he might see. According to verse 17, "the Lord opened the servant's eyes and he saw; and behold, the mountain was full of horses and chariots of fire all around Elisha." The hosts of heaven were invisible, but they were present the whole time.

Conventional wisdom says seeing is believing. The faith principle says believing is seeing.[14]

Another example of this principle is found in the Gospel of Matthew. Hours before the crucifixion, 600 armed men entered the Garden of Gethsemane to arrest Jesus, bringing swords and clubs. One of the disciples, Peter, drew a sword and struck the slave of the high priest, cutting off the man's ear. At this moment, Jesus rebuked Peter, saying, "Put your sword back into its place . . . do you think that I cannot appeal to My Father, and He will at once put at My disposal more than twelve legions of angels?" (Matthew 26:52-53). A legion referred to a fighting unit of up to 6,000 Roman soldiers.[15] Jesus was saying that if He wanted, He could have materialized some 72,000 angels at His side. The disciples couldn't see them, but they were there; they were real.

Faith produces the conviction that invisible things do exist.

Faith and Behavior

For by it the men of old gained approval. (Hebrews 11:2).

The final principle of faith introduced here at the beginning of Hebrews 11 is that *faith prioritizes a lifestyle worthy of commendation.*

The author refers here to Old Testament believers. **Gained approval** means they received great commendation from God and other individuals. Why did they receive such commendation? The verse itself explains: **For by it**—that is, by this kind of faith, by this spiritual trust—the saints of old received commendation. They took the first step, even though they could not see the whole staircase. These **men of old** walked through dark valleys and steep and slippery terrains, and their bodies and minds suffered the consequences. Despite adverse circumstances, they pressed on, clinging with conviction to the reality of invisible things.

They became worthy of the title *heroes.* Though imperfect, they are worth studying, imitating, admiring, and following, as New Testament believers are exhorted to do (cf. Hebrews 6:12; 13:7). In them, we see a living demonstration of faith that provides a foundation upon which we rest our hope, produces conviction of invisible reality, and prioritizes a lifestyle worthy of commendation.

They demonstrated faith that marched to the beat of a different drummer, inviting us to join their ranks and step in line.

By faith we understand that the worlds were prepared by the word of God, so that what is seen was not made out of things which are visible.

–Hebrews 11:3

CHAPTER TWO

THE ULTIMATE, ORIGINAL HERO

Hebrews 11:3

COUNTERFEIT HEROES

Regardless of one's worldview, every human heart intuitively longs to answer six deep existential questions: (1) Is there a God? (2) Where did I come from? (3) Where do I fit in the flow of history? (4) What determines right and wrong? (5) Why do I sometimes feel bad about my actions? (6) What will happen to me after I die?[1]

The naturalistic world fabricates its own answers. Television channels, such as Discovery Channel and Animal Planet, scientific magazines like *National Geographic*, and basically any science textbook answer emphatically that there is no creator God; that we are the result of millions of years of evolutionary processes; that we determine what is right and wrong, and that the bad feelings we have are culturally conditioned.

Entirely consistent with his beliefs, evolutionist Robert Wright espoused this naturalistic viewpoint when he wrote: "There is definitely no reason to assume that existing moral codes reflect some higher truth apprehended via divine inspiration." Wright himself acknowledges the practical consequences of this perspective in matrimony: "Lifelong monogamous devotion just isn't natural."[2] In short, the naturalistic worldview inevitably leads to a lifestyle utterly devoid of any moral principle.

Concerning the third question—Where do I fit in the flow of history?—the unbelieving scientific community advocates that as the most evolved species, the human being is an invader of the planet and actually interferes with the peace and harmony of nature. Based on the answers to the five previous questions, one can only surmise that the answer to the final question—What will happen to me after I die?—brings no hope with it: nothing awaits us after death; the present existence is all there is.[3]

Though at first it might seem that each question is independent of the others, the answers to the last five questions flow down from the first question: Is there a God? If He does exist, then God almost certainly created me. And if so, He has a purpose, a standard of morality, a place in history, and a future for me after death.

Your view of origins determines your view of *everything*.

Early in his life, Charles Darwin often referred to a creator as the one responsible for the formation of a limited number of original forms of life.[4] By 1871, however, God had virtually disappeared from his writings and speculations. In a correspondence with his dear friend Joseph D. Hooker dated February 1, 1871, Darwin wrote: "But if (& oh what a big if) we could conceive in some warm little pond, with all sorts of ammonia and phosphoric salts, —light, heat, electricity etc. present, that a protein compound was chemically formed, ready to undergo still more complex changes...."[5] What Darwin seemed to have neglected is that all those elements whose existence he simply assumed—pond, ammonia, electricity, light, and heat—must have come from somewhere.

Even if we work with the presupposition that these elements were already present, having originated somehow, evolution still faces one huge challenge: the spontaneous generation of complex organic compounds, such as the protein Darwin mentioned. It is extremely unlikely, to say the least, that numerous and complex factors combined all at once, randomly creating the perfect environment for the birth and development of even the simplest organisms.

George D. Wald (1906–97), a scientist awarded the Nobel Prize in medicine (1967) and professor at Harvard University, admitted this when he wrote: "One has only to contemplate the magnitude of this to concede that the spontaneous generation of a living organism is impossible. Yet here we are—as a result, I believe, of spontaneous generation."[6]

If spontaneous generation is impossible, then how can Wald still hold this view? He appeals to *time* as the key factor that makes the impossible not only possible but even certain. Spontaneous generation would be impossible if it had to take place within the space of human lifetime or recorded human history. However, Wald argues, since the phenomenon in question relates to geological time (billions of years), it had a much longer interval of time to take place. It gradually went from being impossible to virtually certain.[7]

In light of Wald's words, it is not hard to capture how essential time is for the naturalistic argument: "Time is the hero of the plot. The time with which we have to deal is of the order of two billion years. What we regard as impossible on the basis of human experience is meaningless here. Given so much time, the 'impossible' becomes possible, the possible becomes probable, and the probable virtually certain. One has only to wait; time itself performs the miracles."[8]

Wald chose time to be his hero.

Darwin, on the other hand, chose for himself a slightly different hero. In a personal letter written to botanist Asa Gray on November 26, 1860, Darwin confessed: "I grieve to say that I cannot honestly go as far as you do about Design. I am conscious that I am in an utterly hopeless muddle. I cannot think that the world, as we see it, is the result of chance; and yet I cannot look at each separate thing as the result of Design . . . Again, I say I am, and shall ever remain, in a hopeless muddle."[9]

Darwin needed a hero to help him out of the muddle. Unfortunately, he chose chance as the hero of history.

Wald chose time to be his hero; Darwin chose chance. They should have heeded the Creator's message preached by powerful expositors of their days. In fact, Darwin lived during the same time and in the same city as Charles Spurgeon and Joseph Parker, preachers who proclaimed biblical truths to thousands every Sunday. As revivals took place in England under the ministry of the visiting American evangelist D. L. Moody, Darwin published his conjectures, explaining life as the result of accidental natural processes without any supernatural interference. And the majority of people rejected the biblical explanation of a creator in favor of Darwin's views.

Throughout history, theories of origins have been crafted as attempts to deny God and still answer life's most basic questions.

HEBREWS 11

THE ORIGINAL HERO

At the very beginning of the list of heroes in Hebrews 11, the author introduces us to the real hero, who is none other than God Himself. He is the ultimate hero of the universe and its history—not chance plus time but God. He is the answer to who we are, where we came from, why we exist, and where our future lies after death.

The first person we encounter in this chapter of heroes is our Creator God.

> **By faith we understand that the worlds were prepared by the word of God, so that what is seen was not made out of things which are visible.** (Hebrews 11:3)

By faith we understand. In other words, our faith makes sense of our world; our faith in a creator clarifies the issue of our origin, purpose, and place. This is the way out of the muddle.

The author did not write, "By faith we *understand* everything." Instead, he wrote that **by faith we understand** that God made everything. The Greek word translated **understand** refers to perception; it means "to perceive with reflective intelligence."[10] In other words, you observe nature around and perceive that there must have been a creator, the same way you look at a watch with its intricate mechanisms and intelligently perceive there was a watchmaker.

Kent Hughes retells the parable of some mice that built a nest and lived inside the bottom of a piano:

> The music of the instrument came to them in their "piano world," filling all the dark spaces with sound and harmony. At first the mice were impressed by it. They drew comfort and wonder from the thought that there was someone who made the music—though invisible to them—someone above, yet close to them. They loved to think of the Great Player whom they could not see.
>
> Then one day a daring mouse climbed up part of the piano and returned very thoughtful. He had found out how the music was made. Wires were the secret—tightly stretched

wires of graduated lengths that trembled and vibrated. They must revise all their old beliefs. None but the most conservative could any longer believe in the Unseen Player. Later another explorer carried the explanation further. Hammers were now the secret—great numbers of hammers dancing and leaping on the wires. This was a more complicated theory, but it all went to show that they lived in a purely mechanical and mathematical world. The Unseen Player came to be thought of as a myth, though the pianist continued to play.[11]

By faith we understand that the worlds were prepared. The word translated **prepared** also means "to outfit, to perfect."[12] Just as you prepare your car before leaving on a vacation, the earth was equipped for life from the very beginning. This means that God created the universe fully prepared and mature in order for it to function properly.

If you traveled back in time to those first six days of creation and arrived just moments after Adam's creation, you would not be introduced to a baby boy, but to a fully-grown man. You would be able to talk to him since he was created with the ability to communicate. If you concluded that Adam was more than one hour old, you would be wrong. He was created fully mature.[13] He was prepared for life.

The same was true for the celestial bodies. The sun, the moon, and the stars were created with their light and properties already benefiting the earth (Genesis 1:14-18). Likewise, God created trees already bearing fruit (Genesis 1:11). Man and animals alike would eat fruits without having to wait a year or more for trees to grow and bear fruit. Just as in the case of man, you would assume that the trees were several years old. An oak tree might already be thirty feet high, providing shade and protection. This means that if you cut it down, you would count the appropriate number of growth rings for an oak tree of that size.[14] The world was fully equipped to sustain the lives of man and animals.

And how did God do it? Was it by means of a long evolutionary process through billions of years? The verse explains: **By faith we understand that the worlds were prepared by the word of God.** The Creator simply spoke the world into existence—fully equipped within a week of days to sustain life. And the more we learn about our planet, the more we recognize how many things needed to exist immediately in order to sustain life.

What naturalism considers to be amazing "coincidences" that make the universe fit for life, Scripture claims to have proceeded from the omniscient and omnipotent mind of God. As Colson and Pearcey put it, "From the molecular properties of water to the balance of electrical charges in the proton and electron, the entire structure of the physical universe is exquisitely designed to support life on Earth."[15] The evidence points emphatically to a Designer.

Some have argued that God created everything necessary for natural developments to take place, thus starting the evolutionary process that ultimately generated life.[16] This view is known as *theistic evolution*, and it is a theory that has been refuted scientifically, philosophically, and theologically.[17] The issue is simply this: Does the Bible teach that God spoke things into existence, which then evolved over billions of years?

The answer is not hard to find. Look further in verse 3: **so that what is seen was not made out of things which are visible.** The author of Hebrews clearly states that God did not use visible things to create the universe and everything in it. He created *ex nihilo*, or "out of nothing." He used preexisting matter only to create and design two beings: Adam and Eve. Adam was crafted out of dirt to remind man that his body will not last forever but will return to the dust. And Eve was created out of Adam's rib to reveal submission *to* him, dependence *upon* him, and at the same time partnership *with* him as one who belongs at his side. The Bible leaves no room for God creating some original ammonia that swam in a warm little pond somewhere, and then programming it to evolve over billions of years. God created all there is—stupendous, complex, vast, and incredible—and to Him it was easy; no effort was necessary.[18]

The psalmist bragged about his Creator, writing:

> By the word of the LORD the heavens were made, and by the breath of His mouth all their host. . . .
>
> Let all the earth fear the LORD; let all the inhabitants of the world stand in awe of Him.

For He spoke, and it was done; He commanded, and it stood fast.

The LORD nullifies the counsel of the nations; He frustrates the plans of the peoples.

The counsel of the LORD stands forever, the plans of His heart from generation to generation.

Blessed is the nation whose God is the LORD, the people whom He has chosen for His own inheritance. (Psalm 33:6, 8-12)

How tragic it is to watch our world erase the signature of the Painter from the mural of His handiwork.

One university educator openly advocated that any professor should have the right to fail a student in his class, no matter what the grade record indicated, if that student defended creationism.[19] Another educator wrote in the *Journal of the National Center for Science Education*, "No advocate of such propaganda [creationism] should be trusted to teach science classes or administer science programs anywhere or under any circumstances. Moreover, if any are now doing so, they should be dismissed."[20]

Any society that refuses even the possibility of a creator God sinks into Darwin's existential "muddle."

The way out of the muddle is this: let God be your ultimate, original hero. When you do so, you discover not only the true answers to those six fundamental questions but also three reassuring principles that follow from Hebrews 11:3.

THREE REASSURING PRINCIPLES

If God's Word Was Sufficient to Equip the Universe to Sustain Life, His Word Is Sufficient to Sustain Your Life

If by simple faith you can trust God concerning what His Word says happened thousands of years ago, you can trust Him as it relates to what happened yesterday, today, and what might happen to you tomorrow. You can trust Him; He has packed your car for the journey He uniquely prepared for you.

If God Knew All the Details Necessary to Create You, He Knows All the Details Necessary to Redeem You

Carl Sagan was a popular evolutionist who promulgated naturalism through his television series and books. He denied the existence of a creator and practically bestowed divine attributes on the universe. He began his television program by saying, "The cosmos is all that is or ever was or ever will be." In a book published near the end of his life, Sagan wrote, "Our planet is a lonely speck in the great enveloping cosmic dark. In our obscurity, in all this vastness, there is no hint that help will come from elsewhere to save us from ourselves."[21] His faith in the absence of God inevitably led him to the despair of utter loss and hopelessness.

Though Sagan never acknowledged this fact, help did come: "In the beginning was the Word, and the Word was with God, and the Word was God. . . . And the Word became flesh, and dwelt among us" (John 1:1, 14). And the Word came to save sinners, for indeed, "as many as received Him, to them He gave the right to become children of God" (John 1:12).

Help came from the only place from which it could come, and from the only One who could offer help—God, who knew all the details when He created us and had planned all the details to redeem us.

As a sinner redeemed by Jesus Christ, you exist by means of God's creative plan, are equipped with a moral compass, are freed from the guilt of the sin you have committed, have a purpose in serving Him, and have a glorious future prepared by Him.

The future will not be so glorious for many, however. In fact, whether sinners acknowledge the truth of the creator God or not, there is a coming day of judgment when the entire world will stand before Him. One day, all will encounter Him face to face. The verdict of the Creator will not be in favor of those who have rejected Him.

William Steig (1907–2003) was a cartoonist, illustrator, and author of award-winning books for children, including *Shrek!* a story that later was turned into a movie. In his children's book entitled *Yellow & Pink*, Steig portrayed the concept of creation and even hinted at the coming encounter of mankind with their Creator. The main characters in the story are Yellow and Pink, two wooden figures who wake up to find themselves lying on an old newspaper in the hot sun. Colson and Pearcey summarize the story and make an important point:

> Suddenly, Yellow sits up and asks, "Do you know what we're doing here?"
>
> "No," replies Pink. "I don't even remember getting here."
>
> So begins a debate between the two marionettes over the origin of their existence.
>
> Pink surveys their well-formed features and concludes, "Someone must have made us."
>
> Yellow disagrees. "I say we're an accident," and he outlines a hypothetical scenario of how it might have happened. A branch might have broken off a tree and fallen on a sharp rock, splitting one end of the branch into two legs. Then the wind might have sent it tumbling down a hill until it was chipped and shaped. Perhaps a flash of lightning struck in such a way as to splinter the wood into arms and fingers. Eyes might have been formed by woodpeckers boring in the wood.
>
> "With enough time, a thousand, a million, maybe two and half million years, lots of unusual things could happen," says Yellow. "Why not us?"
>
> The two figures argue back and forth.
>
> In the end, the discussion is cut short by the appearance of a man coming out of a nearby house. He strolls over to the marionettes, picks them up, and checks their paint. "Nice and dry," he comments, and tucking them under his arm, he heads back toward the house.
>
> Peering out from under the man's arm, Yellow whispers in Pink's ear, "Who is this guy?"

That is precisely the question each one of us must answer, and it's no storybook fantasy. It is deadly serious.[22]

Yellow and Pink are addressing some of those serious existential questions in their own world, but without any revelation from their maker, they can only muse about their origin and purpose. We, on the other hand, have access to the Bible, the special revelation graciously given to us by our good Creator. In it, we have the truth about God, origins, and the future. It contains the answers humanity so desperately seeks to find.

When Paul preached his first message to the scholarly philosophers of Athens in Acts 17, he proclaimed the world as the creation of his God and then announced the coming judgment of the world before God. The seriousness of the biblical doctrine of creation led Francis Schaeffer to remark that if he had only one hour to spend with an unbeliever, he would spend the first fifty-five minutes talking about creation and the last five minutes explaining the way of salvation.[23]

If God Created the Heavens and the Earth, He Is Capable of Creating A New Heaven and A New Earth

When the New Testament refers to creation, it sees it as a past and completed event—an immediate work of God that did not include billions of years in order for the earth to function as it does till this day. When the Bible teaches about the new creation, it speaks of a completed city, with golden streets and gates of pearl.

Many believers have a misconception about the new creation. Since Jesus Christ said in John 14 that He would go and prepare a place for us, some think the work is in progress at the moment—that heaven is under construction, so to speak. But our Lord is not wearing overalls right now; there is no scaffolding in heaven. John the apostle was given a tour two thousand years ago, and everything was finished!

But imagine if an evolutionist were granted a quick trip to heaven. Upon looking at the streets of gold, he would speculate how many gold mines were necessary to lay down that gold pavement and how long it took to refine the gold and then fashion it into sidewalks and streets. He would look at the

THE ULTIMATE, ORIGINAL HERO

gates of pearl, each gate made of a single pearl, and marvel at how long it would have taken the poor oysters to form those pearls!

No, everything was created by the word of God. Genesis, the first book of the Bible, describes this world, and Revelation, the last book, describes the world to come. And that last one will continue forever. We believe these things by faith—faith substantiated by special revelation from God and bolstered by every new scientific discovery as our knowledge regarding nature's incredible complexity and magnificent design expands.

Hebrews 11:3 puts it as simply as it could be delivered to mankind: **By faith we understand that the worlds were prepared** [both this one and the next] **by the word of God, so that what is seen was not made out of things which are visible.** With that, the list of heroes has begun, and the first hero on the list is appropriately the ultimate and original hero: our Creator God.

By faith Abel offered to God a better sacrifice than Cain, through which he obtained the testimony that he was righteous, God testifying about his gifts, and through faith, though he is dead, he still speaks.

–Hebrews 11:4

CHAPTER THREE

BEYOND THE CHERUBIM

Hebrews 11:4

In a bestselling book, the author invited his readers to speak thirty-one declarations over their lives, one each day for a month. He promised that the good things they declared would be guaranteed. The declaration for Day 1 says:

> I DECLARE God's incredible blessings over my life. I will see an explosion of God's goodness, a sudden widespread increase. I will experience the surpassing greatness of God's favor. It will elevate me to a level higher than I ever dreamed of. Explosive blessings are coming my way. This is my declaration.[1]

I wonder how the heroes of faith in Hebrews 11 would define *explosive*. Indeed, their lives stand in stark contrast to the message proclaimed by teachers of false gospels that promise fortune as a result of faith. The first man in God's brochure of testimonials—Abel—was *killed* for his faith.

Hebrews 11 doesn't catalog quick decisions but lifelong disciples. Decisions are easy to make; disciples are hard to make. Decisions take a moment; disciples are forged over a lifetime.

If you've eaten pancakes recently at a restaurant, you were probably given that cheap, thick, artificially colored and artificially sweetened syrup rather than real maple syrup. Pure maple syrup is much more expensive due to the amount of time and effort it takes to make it.

The traditional method of making syrup requires workers to venture deep into the woods they call the "sugar bush." Once they find the maple trees, they use hand drills to make small holes in the trunks of the trees. Afterward, a metal tube (called a *spile*) is carefully tapped into each hole, and a bucket is hung on each spile. The sap then drips slowly into those buckets. It might require fifty trees to yield *forty gallons* of sap—a thin, clear, watery substance with a hint of sweetness. The buckets of sap are poured into large kettles that sit over open fires. The sap comes to a slow boil and, as it boils, the water content is reduced and the sugars are concentrated. Hours later, it has developed a golden-brown color and a rich flavor. The content is strained several times to remove impurities and then reheated all over again. *Forty gallons* of maple sap are necessary to produce just *one gallon* of pure maple syrup. That's why it is so expensive.[2]

Similarly, genuine faith is strained and pressured over time so that impurities may be removed. Afterward, it is heated in the fire and then reheated all over again. Sometimes, such faith never escapes the fire. In Hebrews 11, we find both artificial faith and pure faith. One is quickly made and merely looks the part; the other is costly, having been forged through the trials and pressures of life.

GENUINE FAITH VS. ARTIFICIAL FAITH

By faith Abel offered to God a better sacrifice than Cain, through which he obtained the testimony that he was righteous. (Hebrews 11:4*a*)

The full account of Abel's testimony is found in Genesis 4. However, Genesis 3 provides some important clues to the events surrounding Abel's sacrifice.

Genesis 3 records Adam and Eve's rebellion against God's direct command given in Genesis 2:16-17. They were exposed and confronted by God in the garden for having eaten the forbidden fruit. Following that confrontation, God delivered several curses on His once innocent creation. He cursed the serpent (which is Satan) saying, "And I will put enmity between you and the woman, and between your seed and her seed; he [the seed of the woman] shall bruise you on the head, and you shall bruise him on the heel" (Genesis 3:15).

Although Satan would bruise the followers of this coming Redeemer—and the Redeemer Himself—the damage would only be temporary. The Redeemer, on the other hand, would crush the head of Satan, dealing him a death blow.

Following the curse on the serpent, God delivered His punishment upon Adam and Eve. The sinning couple would now be barred from Paradise, which included intimate fellowship with their creator God. Just before He sent them out of the Garden, we read that "the LORD God made garments of skin for Adam and his wife, and clothed them" (Genesis 3:21).

This was the first act of atonement, when a bloody death became the means of covering the guilt of sin. Adam and Eve had sought to cover their guilt with fig leaves. This was the first religious act in human history—man-made efforts to hide a guilty conscience. God saw through the fig leaves, however, and their sin remained.

Instead of abandoning the couple to their sin and guilt, God provided for them clothing by shedding the blood of an innocent animal. By doing so, He was teaching Adam and Eve that through the bloody death of an innocent animal, their sin would be covered temporarily while they waited for the Coming One who would permanently atone for the guilt of their sin.

Though shamed, cursed, fallen, dejected, crushed, and sorrowful, they responded to the atoning provision of God. They chose to trust God even as they were expelled from the garden. We know this because of Genesis 4:1: "Now the man had relations with his wife Eve, and she conceived and gave birth to Cain, and she said, 'I have gotten a manchild with the help of the LORD.'"

Instead of rebelling in anger and rejecting the atoning plan of God, Eve trusted her Creator and praised Him for the birth of Cain. More than that, she named her son *Cain*, which comes from a word meaning "to acquire" or "get something." Many believe she actually was referring to the earlier promise of a man who would come from her seed to redeem them.[3] She thought Cain was the promised Redeemer.

Unfortunately, Cain would not be mankind's Redeemer; rather, he would become mankind's first murderer. He wouldn't give life; he would take life.

Sometime after the birth of Cain, Eve bore their second son, Abel.

The two boys grew up, and Abel decided to get his major in animal husbandry; Cain decided to major in agriculture. Evidently, as they grew up outside the garden, they were fully aware of their parents' history as well as God's system of sacrifice and atonement. They were also aware of the promised Redeemer.

We know this based on verses 3-4*a*: "So it came about in the course of time that Cain brought an offering to the LORD of the fruit of the ground. Abel, on his part also brought of the firstlings of his flock and of their fat portions." Old Testament scholars believe the phrase "in the course of time" is an expression for some kind of annual event. It can be translated "revolution of days," probably meaning at the end of the year.[4]

The bringing of an offering to God was the standard procedure. Cain and Abel did not come up with this idea on their own; it had been handed down to them by Adam and Eve. The Bible does not reveal the detailed curriculum for their religious education at home, but the actions of these two sons are consistent with an awareness of what God required in this post-garden existence regarding sacrifice.

Likewise, the concept of atonement was not man's idea. The altar was not man's creation, and man did not decide on his own to heap some stones on top of each other, kill an innocent animal, and burn it on the altar. Obviously, God had given to mankind the way to approach Him, and it was through the blood of a sacrifice. Now, this year, perhaps after years of sacrifice, Cain rebelled.

God reacted toward the offerings of the two brothers: "And the LORD had regard for Abel and for his offering; but for Cain and for his offering He had no regard" (Genesis 4:4*b*-5)

Unfortunately, many believe Cain got the short end of the straw. How unlucky can you get? He goes into farming and his brother goes into livestock, and God evidently prefers livestock over fruit and vegetables. Cain must have thought, *I chose the wrong career.*

But that wasn't Cain's problem.

Based on the collation of events found in Genesis 1–5 regarding the ages of Adam and his sons—Cain, Abel, and Seth—Cain was more than 120 years old when the events of Genesis 4 occurred.[5] Abel was not much younger than that. Before the Flood especially, people lived hundreds of years. Adam himself died when he was 930 years old (5:5). So, Cain and Abel were relatively young men in their early 100s.

Cain and Abel had offered individual sacrifices to God perhaps a hundred times or more before the event recorded in Genesis 4. While we cannot be sure how many times Cain and Abel had appeared at the altar with their sacrifices, we know for certain this was not their *first* appearance.

Consequently, we have every reason to believe that this appearance was that moment when Cain essentially said: "I'm tired of getting animals from my brother's herds. I'm just as significant to God as he is! I'm working just as hard as anybody else. This year I'll do it my way. I'll bring all my blue-ribbon fruits and vegetables and offer them on the altar to God."

The Serpent had not gone on vacation. He had been working on Cain for many years with the same strategy he'd used on Cain's mother.

Cain eventually fell for the same line used a century earlier when the Serpent whispered into the ear of Eve, "You can eat the *fruit* of that tree and live your way." Now, the Serpent whispered into Cain's ear, "You can offer the *fruit* of the ground and do it your way."

After approaching God the right way perhaps a hundred times before, this time Cain succumbed to the Serpent's suggestion. In essence, he was saying to himself, "I'll approach God with the work of my own hands. Never mind it is fruit from the ground, which has been cursed. I'm sure God won't mind."

On the surface Genesis 4 and Hebrews 11:4 indicate that both Cain and Abel came at the prescribed time and to the prescribed place of sacrifice. They both appeared to worship God. They both came to the altar, bringing an offering, apparently demonstrating faith that an invisible God would accept their offering.[6] Nonetheless, only one of them had genuine faith. The other's faith was artificial.

- Abel obeyed God's plan of forgiveness; Cain disobeyed God's plan.[7]
- Abel brought what God wanted; Cain brought what he wanted.
- Abel followed divine revelation; Cain followed human reasoning.[8]

Verse 11 of Jude refers to "the way of Cain" in terms of a religious system. Cain becomes the example throughout human history, not of genuine faith, but of a religious system that claims to believe in a higher deity and to be committed to religious works and practices but denies the specific, satisfactory, atoning work of the Messiah who died on a cross. This is the way of Cain: "Let me approach God on *my* own terms; let's avoid all talk of sin, guilt, sacrifice, and the need for a Savior. Let me bring to God what *I* have produced." Cain simply offered to God another version of fig leaves.

The way to God had been barred since the fall of man in the garden of Eden. Through all the Old Testament and up to the cross of Christ, the doorway to God was under lock and key. Only one key could unlock the door and allow free, unrestricted worship of our Creator.

GENUINE FAITH: UNLOCKING ACCESS TO GOD

When Cain and Abel presented their offerings in Genesis 4, the altar already existed, having been used for more than a century. Cain and Abel not only had a prescribed time to worship and confess (annually) and a prescribed manner in which to approach God (through animal sacrifice), but they also had a *place* to worship Him.

When Adam and Eve left the garden, God assigned *cherubim* (warrior angels) to guard the entrance. More specifically, according to Genesis 3:24, they would guard the entrance to the garden on the east side, thus preventing mankind from accessing Paradise again. Many believe this was the place where Adam and Eve, and later their sons, went to offer the prescribed atoning sacrifices to God. After all, at this east gate stood the cherubim and their flaming sword. This was the place that marked their exile, where the curse had been delivered, along with the promise of a Redeemer.

We are not informed about how long these cherubim stood at the east gate of the garden of Eden; they may have done so until the catastrophic Flood wiped mankind off the face of the earth (Genesis 6–9) and reshaped the topography of the planet, thus causing the garden to disappear. But even after the Flood, God kept alive the memory of the fall of man, the resulting exile of mankind from Paradise, and the cherubim that barred the entrance to the garden.

It is no coincidence that in the Israelite Levitical system, both in the tabernacle and later in the temple, the priests would approach God from the east side.

When Israel departed from Egypt under the leadership of Moses, God gave directions for the construction of the tabernacle—a moveable meeting place. This tent was divided into two major areas: the Holy Place and the Holy of Holies.

Priests were allowed to enter the Holy Place just outside the Holy of Holies in order to perform a number of sacred duties unto God. As it concerns the Holy of Holies, on the other hand, there were more restrictions. It was in the Holy of Holies that rested the ark of the covenant—a golden box that initially contained the tablets of the law delivered to Moses at Mount Sinai. This was the place of God's unique presence. On the lid of the ark, which was called the mercy seat, were golden figures of cherubim, one on each end (Exodus 25:17-22).

A heavy curtain separated the Holy Place from the Holy of Holies. According to God's commands in Exodus 26, figures of cherubim were to be embroidered into the fabric of that curtain. The cherubim still guarded access to God. The best God's people could do was to sacrifice to Him from a distance.

Later when the magnificent temple was built, huge cherubim figures were sewn into the curtain to signify that access was restricted. In addition, a pair of sculpted cherubim guarded the entrance to the inner sanctuary (1 Kings 6:23-28). They were fifteen feet high, and their wings spread out another fifteen feet—huge, imposing, impressive. The message from the garden of Eden was alive and well, as though God said: "You cannot come in here, but you can sacrifice nearby."

Only one man was allowed to enter the Holy of Holies: the high priest. He entered the room in trembling fear on the Day of Atonement (Leviticus 16). Bearing in his hands the blood of an innocent animal, the high priest would slip between the folds of that curtain embroidered with the warrior angels. Once inside the Holy of Holies, he would face directly the ark of the covenant.

It was impossible not to be awestruck by the cherubim sculptures that guarded the presence of God. Mankind was still barred from free and open access.

But the priest would sprinkle the blood on the mercy seat, and God would *temporarily* be satisfied with the covering of the sins of the nation. This temporary covering pointed to a wooden altar upon which the Lamb of God would die and end all sacrifices once and for all. Just before He died, our Redeemer cried out, "It is finished!" (John 19:30).

And what happened then? That curtain in the temple nearby was ripped from top to bottom as if God the Father Himself said, "The door is permanently unlocked. There are no more cherubim barring entrance to personal confession and fellowship with the living God."

We can now do much better than the high priest. We can go between and beyond the cherubim to the very throne of God anytime we wish. And even now, all believers can walk with God in fellowship with their Savior and Lord.

Horatius Bonar wrote a hymn that captures well the essence of all this:

> *Not what these hands have done*
> *Can save this guilty soul;*
> *Not what my toiling flesh has borne*
> *Can make my spirit whole. . . .*
>
> *Thy work alone, O Christ,*
> *Can ease this weight of sin;*
> *Thy blood alone, O Lamb of God,*
> *Can give me peace within.*[9]

GENUINE FAITH: RECEIVING GOD'S APPROVAL

God testifying about his gifts. (Hebrews 11:4*b*)

The narrative in Genesis 4 continues and shows how God received the offerings of the two brothers: "And the LORD had regard for Abel and for his offering; but for Cain and for his offering He had no regard" (Genesis 4:4*b*-5*a*). The writer of Hebrews expands on this by writing that **God** [was]

testifying about his [Abel's] **gifts** (Hebrews 11:4). This sentence can be rendered "God testified over his gifts."

This strongly suggests that God performed something obvious to everyone that showed He received Abel's offering but rejected Cain's offering. What exactly did God do to declare this publicly?

Though we are not told specifically, by comparing Scriptures, it seems likely that something dramatic happened at each annual sacrifice. Throughout the Old Testament, God proved in a visible way His acceptance of both the offering and the offerer:

- He sent fire from heaven and consumed Aaron's offering upon the altar (Leviticus 9:24).

- The Angel of the Lord sent fire to consume Gideon's sacrifice (Judges 6:21).

- God sent fire from heaven to consume Elijah's offering when His prophet confronted the worshippers of Baal on Mount Carmel (1 Kings 18:38).

- God sent fire from heaven upon the altar when king David offered solemn sacrifices to the Lord (1 Chronicles 21:26).

- Fire came down from heaven and consumed the sacrifices of praise Solomon offered to God at the dedication of the temple (2 Chronicles 7:1).

Fire from heaven was God's testimony of acceptance. It is likely that year after year, as Adam and Eve came to the edge of the garden along with their sons to sacrifice on that altar within sight of the cherubim who guarded everything they had lost, the Lord in His grace testified to their faith by sending fire from heaven to consume their offerings.

This year, however, things were different. There stood the two brothers. The fire fell. Abel's gift was consumed, and Cain's produce remained untouched. It was utter humiliation and public embarrassment for Cain. More than likely, the Serpent whispered into Cain's ear, "This is blatant favoritism! You're just as good as he is!"

The envy in the heart of Cain began to grow, and it eventually blazed into murderous hatred. He became history's first murderer and his younger brother became the first martyr, dying because of his genuine faith.

HEBREWS 11

GENUINE FAITH: PROCLAIMING TRUTH FROM THE DEAD

And through faith, though he is dead, he still speaks.
(Hebrews 11:4c)

Abel's martyrdom was not the last word. Hebrews uses his example to teach us that when we live in obedience to the Word of God, our life might not get easier; it might get more difficult. The walk of faith may lead us directly into the valley of the shadow of death. Abel did what was right and was hated for it. He worshipped God correctly and was persecuted for it. He obeyed God and was murdered for it.

The testimony of Abel also proclaims that there is only one way to God and only one foundation for genuine faith. Without the shedding of blood, the curtain stays closed, the cherubim remain on guard and the gate to Paradise remains locked.

Based on our fuller, New Testament understanding of God's redemptive plan—of which Abel knew only a fraction—Abel's faith said this: Jesus paid it all. Everything else is fig leaves and the religion of Cain. It might taste sweet and look like syrup. It might even be labeled genuine, but it remains artificial. Jesus Christ and faith in Him alone is the genuine sweetness of pure faith.

Abel stood at the altar, with the two cherubim and the flashing sword nearby barring the gate to Paradise lost. He acknowledged God's right to exile him. He also acknowledged he was a sinner who needed atonement. He offered his sacrifice and the fire fell. This was a testimony of both God's pleasure and the core of the gospel—that the seed of the woman, the coming Redeemer, would feel the fire of God the Father's wrath upon Him. Because of His sacrifice, access to Paradise and to the throne of God would be reopened.

Abel, the first human hero of faith, begins the legacy of genuine faith. He practiced outside the garden what Christ would say inside the garden where He prayed: "Not My will, but Yours be done" (Luke 22:42). Hours later, Jesus Christ submitted to an altar of wood and separation from the Father to complete the plan of redemption.

Abel's sacrifice was one lamb for one person, a shadow of things to come.

Later came the Passover—one lamb for one family.

Later still came the annual sacrifice on the Day of Atonement—one lamb for one nation.

Finally, the Messiah came, the seed of the woman, and gave His life as the once-for-all sacrifice for sin—one Lamb for the entire world.

And those who come to God as He prescribes, through faith and trust in the sacrifice of His Son, can gladly sing:

> *My faith has found a resting place,*
> *Not in device nor creed;*
> *I trust the ever living One,*
> *His wounds for me shall plead.*
> *I need no other argument,*
> *I need no other plea,*
> *It is enough that Jesus died,*
> *And that He died for me.*[10]

⁵By faith Enoch was taken up so that he would not see death; AND HE WAS NOT FOUND BECAUSE GOD TOOK HIM UP; *for he obtained the witness that before his being taken up he was pleasing to God. ⁶And without faith it is impossible to please Him, for he who comes to God must believe that He is and that He is a rewarder of those who seek Him.*

–Hebrews 11:5–6

CHAPTER FOUR

THE FIRST TO VANISH

Hebrews 11:5-6

At funerals we often hear people trying to make meaning out of the deceased's life. Sometimes the glowing statements about that person leave us wondering if we've wandered into the wrong funeral! At moments like this, however, we are confronted with what matters most.

We never hear eulogies such as, "I never saw him drive a used car," "She always wore designer clothes," or "You should have seen her kitchen." The ones present look for evidence that the deceased person knew and lived for what really mattered in life.

For Christians, what matters most is that we walk with God.

The Lord knew we would need help to understand what it means to walk with God, so He provided an example made of flesh and blood, a hero of living faith who left that kind of legacy for us.

HE WHO VANISHED

His name is Enoch. He appears in three different passages of Scripture: Genesis 5:18-24; Hebrews 11:5-6; and verses 14-15 of the book of Jude. From these three passages we can reconstruct Enoch's personal biography chronologically.

HEBREWS 11

The Seventh Generation from Adam

The first piece of information comes from the epistle of Jude: "It was also about these men that Enoch, in the seventh generation from Adam, prophesied" (Jude 14*a*). Why mention that Enoch was the seventh generation from Adam? Are we supposed to be impressed by his pedigree? Was he the distant relative of a prominent king or ruler?

A study of the descendants of Adam shows that Enoch came from a godly line of believers. He was the seventh patriarch descending from the line of Seth, the son of Adam. His particular place in the genealogy is the counterpart to the seventh generation from the line of Cain, another son of Adam. The seventh patriarch in the line of Cain was Lamech, and there is a striking contrast between Enoch and Lamech.

Genesis 4 lists the descendants of Cain, along with some of their accomplishments, while Genesis 5 lists the descendants of Seth. The two family lines can be confusing because both lines have sons named Enoch and Lamech. However, Seth and his descendants represent a godly line of believers, of which Enoch is in the seventh generation. Cain and his descendants are described as ungodly.

Lamech, the descendant of Cain, was the epitome of wickedness, a man who boasted about killing a young boy for striking him (Genesis 4:23). He bragged that he was many times more vengeful than his forefather, Cain, the first murderer in human history (verse 24). Also, with Lamech we find the first record of a man who practiced polygamy, thus violating the God-created ideal for marriage. Thus, Lamech represented the fallen corruption of man: he was a self-centered, brutal, immoral man who defied the authority of God.

With this background, one can conclude that Jude, by including the detail that Enoch was in the seventh generation from Adam, reminds us that Enoch's life ran parallel to Lamech's. This, in turn, informs us that Enoch lived during days of rampant evil.

Enoch represents those who follow God; Lamech represents those who defy God. Enoch defines the person heading to heaven; Lamech defines the one heading to hell. Enoch represents eternal justification; Lamech represents eternal judgment.

The Patriarch Who Prophesied the Coming Judgment

This same "Enoch, in the seventh generation from Adam, prophesied, saying, 'Behold, the Lord came with many thousands of His holy ones, to execute judgment upon all, and to convict all the ungodly of all their ungodly deeds which they have done in an ungodly way, and of all the harsh things which ungodly sinners have spoken against Him'" (Jude 14-15).

Here Jude also provides the second clue for reconstructing Enoch's biography. The half brother of Jesus writes that this pre-flood patriarch prophesied that the Lord would come with thousands of His holy ones to execute judgment upon all the ungodly because of their sins.

We know from the record of Revelation that this judgment will take place at the end of the tribulation when Christ returns with His church to judge the world and establish His earthly kingdom. We have every reason to believe that Enoch didn't know how distant that future judgment was. He just knew it was coming. In fact, another worldwide judgment would arrive much sooner.

The Father of Methuselah

Another piece of Enoch's biography is found in Genesis 5: "Enoch lived sixty-five years, and became the father of Methuselah" (verse 21). There's more to this story than at first meets the eye.

According to Jude 14, Enoch was a prophet from God and the content of his prophecy was eschatological—that is, it dealt with the still future end times. The Genesis narrative also indicates that he received specific revelation about a coming judgment. This revelation, however, was not about the end times. It was linked to an earlier judgment, and it caused Enoch to name his son "Methuselah."

The name Methuselah is elusive and informative at the same time. Its meaning is extremely difficult to determine, but many linguists perceive a possible reference to *javelin*, or *dart*. Based on the construction of the name, it is possible to suggest it means "man of the javelin"[1] and thus could refer to a coming judgment. But there is another possible meaning of the name, which I believe is accurate: "When he is dead, it [i.e., judgment] shall be sent."[2] It seems Enoch the prophet received from God a revelation that he would preach to his generation this specific warning: God is going to send judgment on the present world.

Scholars disagree about certain aspects of the genealogy of Genesis 5, especially whether there are gaps between some of the generations. According to God's revelation of beginnings—which is what the word *Genesis* means—Adam was created in the first year of creation, specifically on the sixth day. Adam then lived for 930 years. Many believe that in the days before the Flood, a water canopy in the atmosphere shielded the earth from harmful rays and the planet was watered daily by heavy dew. This would have allowed humans to live very long lives. Whether this is the mechanism God used or not, the Bible is clear that people lived for centuries prior to the Flood.

Continuing in Genesis 5, we discover that Enoch's father, Jared, was born 460 years after Adam. There is no doubt that Jared and Adam knew each other. All these patriarchs were well aware of one another. Then Enoch was born. Compared to the rest of the men in the list, Enoch's life on the earth ended when he was still very young, at the age of 365.

At the young age of sixty-five, Enoch and his wife had their first child—a son. And although Scripture gives no details, God visited Enoch in some fashion and informed him of coming judgment. And He also may well have informed him that his son's life would measure God's final years of patience: when this boy died, God would pour out His judgment on the human race. God may have said: "Name your son *Methuselah* because he will become a living demonstration of his name: 'When he dies, judgment will come.'"

Is that what happened? According to the genealogy of Genesis 5, Noah is the *last patriarch* on the list. The clues of this chronology place his birth in the year 1056. Scripture also tells us he lived 950 years—600 years before the Flood and 350 years after the flood (Genesis 9:28-29). This allows us to date the actual event of the Flood to the very year it happened—1656 years after creation. And that happens to be *the same year Methuselah died.*

Can you imagine being Enoch, holding his newborn son and hearing from God that Methuselah's life would be the length of God's fuse? As long as the boy lived, the judgment tarried.[3] And Methuselah lived on—a lot more than a few months or years. He lived 969 years.

When Methusaleh turned 850, God commanded Noah to begin building an ark. As Methuselah grew older, Noah and his family grew busier. They worked on the ark, inside and outside, until the day Noah hung the door on the hinges of that massive boat and packed it with food and supplies. As Methuselah turned 969 years old, perhaps he saw animals beginning to appear in pairs as the ark was finished. Noah's family may even have been getting on board when they heard the news: "Grandpa Methuselah has died."

Every patriarch from the line of Seth had now passed away, except for Noah. The judgment of God, promised nearly a thousand years earlier, arrived. For the first time in human history, the sound of thunder was heard and rain began to fall.

Methuselah never reserved a seat on the ark because he knew he didn't need to. His death would signal the judgment of God. He had been a living illustration of God's mercy and patience.

Is it not interesting that the man whose death would introduce God's judgment was the man that God determined would live longer than any other human being in history? That's how patient God is with unbelieving mankind.

Keep in mind that no record indicates that Enoch knew how long his son would live. I'm sure he would have been surprised to know that Methuselah would live 969 years. As far as he knew, his son might die in infancy.

As early as Genesis 5, the human race was involved in demonic and astral worship, living in utter rebellion and depravity, marked by violence and sin. Men boasted about killing children; polygamy and sexual abuses of women were in vogue. Enoch must have been thinking, *My son isn't going to live for very long.* As far as he knew, his son might live two months or perhaps two years.

The Man Who Walked with God

The remarkable thing about the birth of Methuselah was the radical change it made in the life of Enoch. Like surviving a gunshot wound, cancer, or bankruptcy, the birth of Methuselah dramatically altered the life of Enoch forever. From the moment he held little Methuselah in his arms, he was a different man.

God wants to make sure we don't miss the crossroads experience in Enoch's life: "*Then* Enoch walked with God three hundred years *after* he became the father of Methuselah" (Genesis 5:22). His entire outlook on life completely changed.

That's a good thing for every man who becomes a father. This is the moment you're struck with the fact that you're now responsible for the next generation. You will be watched. You will be modeled. You will need to walk with God like never before.

This reminds me of the testimony of a man who struggled with alcoholism, and nothing could get him to stop—not the financial struggles, the pleading of his wife, or the disrepair of their home. Then they had a little boy. But it wasn't the boy's birth that impacted this man's heart. It was something that happened one winter day.

After this father slammed the door of their house and headed through the snow toward a nearby tavern, he heard behind him his little boy calling out, "Daddy, slow down! Daddy, slow down!" The father turned around and saw his son taking giant steps to step where his father had stepped.

He shouted to his son, "Go back inside! What are you doing?"

The little boy said, "Look at me, Daddy! I'm big enough now to walk in your footprints."

The father was thunderstruck with guilt. He walked over, picked up his son, and headed back toward the house, saying more to himself than to his son, "Well, in that case, I had better change direction."

Enoch was from the godly line of Seth. He already followed God. We would call him a *believer* in our vernacular. He wasn't an idolater. In fact, no one would have been surprised to see that God chose him to be one of the prophetic voices in the land.

In his commentary on Genesis, Kent Hughes points out that the Old Testament distinguishes between people who walked *before* God, those who walked *after* God, and those who walked *with* God—that is, by the side of God.[4] There's just the slightest implied difference between walking *after* God and walking *with* God. They can be the same thing, but they might imply something different, something deeper.

We're not told what issues changed in Enoch's life and heart, but before the birth of his son, his epitaph would not have read, "He walked with God." After Methuselah's birth, whatever the obstruction was to spiritual communion—whether a lack of desire and passion, potential compromise, or rebellion—Enoch evidently dealt with it. He not only began to walk *after* God and *before* God, but he also began a close, intimate walk *with* God.

What Does It Take to Walk with God?

Walking with God requires the same basic decisions we must make in order to walk with anyone else.[5]

First, we have to agree on the destination. If you want to walk around the block five times and I want to walk to a restaurant for cake and sweet tea, we have to go our separate ways—I'm going to feel sorry for you. We can't walk together unless we walk in the same direction. We must have the same purpose, the same goal, in mind.

Second, we have to keep the same speed or pace. Suppose I ring your doorbell and say, "Hey, how about a walk around the block?" You answer, "Sure." Then while you are getting your shoes on, I add, "I'll go ahead and get started." But if you walked around the block ten steps behind me, we might be out on the street at the same time, but we're not in conversation; we're not enjoying each other's fellowship. We're in the same neighborhood, but we're not walking together.

In order to walk with someone, you need to have the same purpose in your spirit and the same pace in your step.

Something evidently happened to Enoch's purpose and pace.

THE FAITH OF HE WHO VANISHED

And without faith it is impossible to please Him, for he who comes to God must believe that He is and that He is a rewarder of those who seek Him. (Hebrews 11:6)

According to Hebrews 11, Enoch began to exercise living, passionate faith from two distinct perspectives.

Enoch Began to Trust That God Really Exists

Without trusting God as it concerns our purpose and pace in life, we can't have close communion with Him. The author is writing to believers, so *saving* faith is not in view. What is in view is the sanctifying faith that finds close fellowship with God the greatest treasure in life.

What kind of faith is that? It is the faith that believes God exists: **for he who comes to God must believe that He is**. Don't all Christians believe that? Sure they do. The question is: Do we who believe it act like it? Do we really acknowledge Him in all our ways and lean upon Him for wisdom, or do we act like He probably isn't in our neighborhood, so we walk at our own pace and for our own purpose and hope God will be okay with that?

Have you ever been around a Christian for some time talking to him and then walk away thinking to yourself, *Man, that guy really believes God is alive*? Enoch was that kind of person. He believed God really exists, and he walked like it.

Enoch Began to Trust That God Is Actually Involved

Enoch no doubt was mocked for his commitment. He faithfully walked with God for three hundred years, proclaiming the truth, but his society only grew more depraved. Then Noah began to build an ark, picking up where Enoch had left off, presenting an evangelistic message. The evangelistic careers of these men of God lasted a total of more than four hundred years. The results? *None* whatsoever.

The readers of Hebrews would be wondering if remaining pure, pursuing a walk with God, and maintaining a distinctive testimony in the midst of a depraved culture was really worth the effort: "Is God really alive and in control? Is He really aware of our situation?"

Often, that is precisely the secret struggle in our own hearts: "Lord, are You there? Have You noticed what's going on in my life? Do you even care?"

Every sincere Christian wants to strengthen his walk with Christ; he wants to commune with Christ and be pleasing to Him. But how do we grow stronger in our faith? How do we strengthen our legacy of faith in walking with God? Begin to practice these two perspectives: live as if God is truly alive, and act as if God is actually involved in the events of your life.

Thomas Manton, a Puritan pastor who ministered in the late 1800s, wrote a devotional commentary on Hebrews 11 based on his sermons. He offered some practical advice on how to strengthen your faith in one section of his book he entitled, "How to work up your faith."

First, he said, you strengthen your walk of faith by *meditation*. He wrote, "There is nothing that you prize but your mind will run upon." In other words, think about Christ; think about heaven and your happiness there; think about the glory and beauty of your future with Him. Imagine it!

A second way to build up your faith is by *argumentation*. This doesn't mean to go out and pick a fight. Manton meant to actually argue with yourself whenever you wonder or doubt. Get into the Word and commit your mind to the truth of God's promises. Argue with anything that rises up against the hope you have within you. When was the last time you had a good argument with yourself?

Third, Manton recommended *supplication*. Pray the Psalms and cry out with the psalmist, "Oh, Lord! Guide me with Your counsel. Let Your truth and Your light lead me" (Psalm 73:24; 43:3 paraphrased).

Fourth, he said you can "work up" your faith through *spiritual diligence*. People strive and war to step higher in the world. They rise early and go to bed late, only to maintain their frail lives that are crumbling to dust. Shall we do nothing for God? Should we not be more industrious than we are?

Fifth, *expectation* is a means of strengthening your walk of faith. Look for the Lord, and long for His appearing, just as the believers on the island of Crete were exhorted to look "for the blessed hope and the appearing of the glory of our great God and Savior, Christ Jesus" (Titus 2:13).[6]

This kind of life, by the way, doesn't pull you away from people; it doesn't lead you into isolation like some ascetic who withdraws from the world and the normal pressures of life and relationships.[7] On the contrary, Enoch began to passionately engage with his generation precisely *because* of his walk of faith.

THE ENDURING LEGACY OF HE WHO VANISHED

By faith Enoch was taken up so that he would not see death; AND HE WAS NOT FOUND BECASUE GOD TOOK HIM UP; for he obtained the witness that before his being taken up he was pleasing to God. (Hebrews 11:5)

This is not only the final piece of Enoch's biography but also his enduring legacy. Enoch was the first person to supernaturally vanish from the earth. The Greek verb *metatithēmi*, translated here taken up, is used in both biblical and extrabiblical literature to convey the idea of change or alteration.

It means to transfer or bring to another place and in this context means Enoch was taken to another location. The same Greek verb is used here as is used in the Septuagint to translate the Hebrew text of Genesis 5:24, which tells that God *took* Enoch to Himself.[8]

Enoch suddenly vanished. We're not told how God did it. All we know is that He did it.

Warren Wiersbe writes, "Enoch had been walking with God for so many years that his transfer to heaven was not even an interruption."[9] His legacy is that he so walked *with* God that he eventually walked *away* with God.

The text indicates Enoch couldn't be found. This suggests that people sent out search parties. Some of Enoch's family no doubt suspected foul play from the line of Cain:[10] "Who saw him last? Where was he before he disappeared? This doesn't just happen!"

But some day the same thing will happen again, only this time every person who has placed his or her faith in Jesus Christ will suddenly vanish from the earth, snatched up to meet the Lord in the air at the rapture (1 Thessalonians 4:13-18). There will be no funerals for those believers; like Enoch, they will never experience death.

Enoch not only became a prophet of the coming judgment from God upon the earth, but he also became the first to experience God's ability to move someone from earth to heaven "in the twinkling of an eye" (1 Corinthians 15:52).

G. Campbell Morgan, the outstanding Bible expositor of the last century, recounted the story of a little girl who came home from Sunday school after hearing the story of Enoch.

She told her mother, "We heard about a wonderful man today in Sunday school." The sensible mother let her child tell what she had heard. "His name was Enoch. And you know, Mother, he used to go for walks with God."

The mother responded, "That's wonderful. But how does the story end?"

The girl replied, "Oh, one day they walked on and on and got so far that God said to Enoch, 'You are a long way from home, now. You might as well come on to My home and stay with Me.'"[11]

So ends the biography of a man who left us a legacy of faith, a man who modeled what it means to walk with God and to literally walk *away* with God.

This is God's plan for us as well. Every one of us who belongs to Him will one day end our walk of faith when our Lord invites us to just come on to His house and live with Him forever.

By faith Noah, being warned by God about things not yet seen, in reverence prepared an ark for the salvation of his household, by which he condemned the world, and became an heir of the righteousness which is according to faith.

–Hebrews 11:7

CHAPTER FIVE

FLEEING THE CITY OF DESTRUCTION

Hebrews 11:7

John Bunyan was a Baptist pastor in England during the difficult days of Charles II, when there was little to no religious liberty in England. This monarch closed down houses where independent meetings took place; religious services were allowed only within the state church.

Bunyan was unwilling to conform to this rule. Because of his persistence in preaching without a government license, he ended up spending several years in the Bedford prison for what he called "conscience' sake." At one point, officials promised to release him if he would stop preaching. John's now famous response was: "If you let me out today, I will be preaching tomorrow."

God had a greater plan for Bunyan's influence. It was while serving two different prison sentences that he wrote his classic work entitled *The Pilgrim's Progress*.

In his opening lines, Bunyan describes the conviction of young Pilgrim, which led to his escape from the city of Destruction:

> I saw a man clothed with rags, standing in a certain place, with . . . a book in his hand, and a great burden upon his back. . . . I looked and saw him open the book, and read therein; and as he read, he wept and trembled . . . and as he

read, he burst out, as he had done before, crying, "What shall I do to be saved?" . . . I looked then, and saw a man named Evangelist coming to him, and he asked, "Wherefore dost thou cry?" . . . Then said Evangelist, "If this be thy condition, why standest thou still?" He answered, "Because I know not whither to go." Then he gave him a parchment roll, and there was written within, "Fly from the wrath to come." . . . Then said Evangelist, (pointing with his finger over a very wide field,) "Do you see yonder wicket-gate?" The man said, "No." Then said the other, "Do you see yonder shining light?" He said, "I think I do." Then said Evangelist, "Keep that light in your eye, and go up directly thereto, so shalt thou see the gate; at which, when thou knockest, it shall be told thee what thou shalt do." So I saw in my dream that the man began to run. Now he had not run far from his own door when his wife and children, perceiving it, began to cry after him to return; but the man put his fingers in his ears, and ran on crying, "Life! life! eternal life!" So he looked not behind him, but fled towards the middle of the plain.[1]

John Bunyan describes how two neighbors ran after him to catch him and bring him back by force. Instead, Christian—which was the name of this pilgrim—told them, "You are dwelling in the city of Destruction . . . be content, good neighbors, and come along with me." Eventually, following one adventure after another, Christian escaped the City of Destruction and safely entered the Celestial City of God.

FAITH ACCORDING TO PROFESSOR NOAH

Nearly everyone in England and America for more than three hundred years owned a copy of *The Pilgrim's Progress*. The story of Christian's escape from future judgment and his invitation for others to join him powerfully delivered the gospel.

In Hebrews 11:7, we see something strikingly similar:

By faith Noah, being warned by God about things not yet seen, in reverence prepared an ark for the salvation of his household, by which he condemned the world, and became an heir of the righteousness which is according to faith.

This verse introduces us to a man who effectively plugged his ears and ignored the culture of ridicule, anger, rejection, sin, and temptation around him. He spent 120 years building an ark while telling his world: "Judgment is coming. Escape along with me!"

Most often, we connect the heroes of the Bible primarily to one event or moment in their lives. For example, we think of Daniel and the lion's den, Jonah and the great fish, and Noah and the ark.

Frankly, we should immediately think of Noah and his *faith*. He is the only hero listed in Hebrews 11 whose biography begins and ends with a reference to his faith.

Four principles of faith emerge as Noah literally escaped from the coming judgment.

Faith Is Demonstrated by Personal Profession in the Midst of Unbelief

Verse 7 opens by recording: **By faith Noah, being warned by God about things not yet seen**. One of those **things not yet seen** was precisely the coming judgment of God upon an incredibly wicked world.

It was in the days of Noah that the once godly line of Seth was corrupted by violent and wicked men who were also obsessed with occultism and sexual perversion. The heroes of that generation were admired because of their strength, power, and wicked domination of others. The testimony of Noah's generation appears in Genesis 6:5: "Then the LORD saw that the wickedness of man was great on the earth, and that every intent of the thoughts of his heart was only evil continually."

Several biblical passages refer to the condition of the world before the flood, thus providing an accurate portrait of the people and society of Noah's day:

- Total disregard for the marriage covenant (Genesis 4:19)

- Rapid advancement in technology (Genesis 4:22)
- Widespread violence and the devaluing of human life (Genesis 4:23)
- A population explosion (Genesis 6:1)
- Rampant evil (Genesis 6:5)
- Immorality and corruption as normative patterns within human relationships (Genesis 6:12)
- Preoccupation with temporary matters (Luke 17:27)
- Materialism (Luke 17:28)
- Rejection of the authority of God's Word (1 Peter 3:18-20)
- No concern for God in either belief or conduct (2 Peter 2:5)[2]

These were the days of Noah. The similarities to our world today are striking.

Just one example is a television show that broke new ground some time ago. The plot revolved around a homosexual couple who enjoy (as NBC advertised) a committed and loving partnership that lacks only one thing: a baby. So, the homosexual couple seeks out a single woman to be a surrogate mother so they can have their baby. The media world was full of excitement with praise and accolades and predictions of Emmy awards in future days.

It's no secret that the world at large is eager and ready to applaud anyone who "breaks new ground." After all, this is just a synonym for breaking up the ground instituted by the creator God.

Against the gloomy background of such a broken world shines the remarkable life of Noah. Right in the middle of all this debauchery and evil, we find his amazing testimony: "Noah walked with God" (Genesis 6:9). And in his world, that meant he walked alone.

Like Christian in Bunyan's *The Pilgrim's Progress*, he was the only one willing to believe that sinners will face the coming judgment of God, unless they escape through the wicket gate and up the hill to the cross. In the middle of this dark night of wickedness flickered the candle of one solitary man who walked with God.

Noah's generation had their list of "heroes"—"men of renown," the Emmy winners of his day (Genesis 6:4). Noah wasn't one of them. Living faith is more interested in the approval of God than the applause of men.[3]

Faith Is Demonstrated by Patience in the Midst of Silence

Noah acted in obedience when **warned by God**, even **about things not yet seen**. Believers in general, and perhaps especially those well acquainted with the narratives of Scripture, tend to underestimate the task to which God called Noah simply because they know the end of the story. Noah was called to believe that something unlikely—something that had never happened before—would happen.

It is staggering that after the initial instructions, Noah worked without any further word from God.[4] In Genesis 6, God commanded Noah to build the ark because of the coming judgment of the earth by means of the flood. And that was it. It appears that God was silent for the next hundred years.

God finally broke the silence in Genesis 7, when He told Noah to gather his family and enter the ark with the animals and wait there in the ark for seven more days. Those additional days of silence must have felt like another hundred years.

The door of the ark was shut and then nothing happened—one day, two days, three days, four days . . . not one drop of rain. We can only imagine the "Noah jokes" as the neighbors' blasphemy against Noah's God only increased.

And then, gentle raindrops began to dance off the sand. Suddenly, the springs of water under the earth erupted, and the judgment of God fell on planet Earth and the entire human race.

Noah was right after all. By faith, he worked and waited in obedience to God, who for the most part remained silent.

Faith Is Demonstrated by Personal Piety in the Midst of Uncertainty

Hebrews 11:7 says that **in reverence** Noah **prepared an ark for the salvation of his household**. This third principle of faith is anchored in Noah's attitude as conveyed by the Greek word translated **in reverence**. It is often translated "holy fear." This wasn't fear, but "sweet reverence" and "devotional awe" of God. He had a "reverent heart . . . in a dark world."[5]

How dark? The number of people following the standard of God for morality, integrity, relationships, and marriage, had dwindled down to *one* family.[6]

Only one family got on that ark, even though the whole world was invited. After Noah preached for 120 years, not one family beyond his own believed his message.

According to the writer of Hebrews, Noah was **warned by God about things not yet seen**. A more detailed analysis of the passages of Scripture surrounding this hero of faith reveals that Noah received not only the disclosure of God's judgment but also the *details* of God's judgment. We find the specifics in Genesis 6.

Genesis 6:14-22 covers 120 years of Noah's life (see 6:3). The reason I've entitled this principle of faith "Piety in the Midst of Uncertainty" is simply because everything God commanded Noah to accomplish was entirely foreign to him. Noah was asked to do things he had absolutely no experience in doing.

God will use a farmer (9:20) to build the largest ship known to mankind. Once completed, it would have weighed more than 18,000 tons, sitting in Noah's pasture.

Genesis 6:13-14 records:

> Then God said to Noah, "The end of all flesh has come before Me; for the earth is filled with violence because of them; and behold, I am about to destroy them with the earth. Make for yourself an ark of gopher wood; you shall make the ark with rooms, and shall cover it inside and out with pitch.

Then God emphasized the extent of His coming judgment in verse 17:

> "Behold, I, even I am bringing the flood of water upon the earth, to destroy all flesh in which is the breath of life, from under heaven; everything that is on the earth shall perish."

Taking God's words at face value, the flood would cover the earth and kill everything that breathed. Only marine life would survive outside the ark.

According to the dimensions given for its construction, this ark was 450 feet long, about 75 feet wide, and 45 feet high. As a way of comparison, that's one and a half football fields long, nearly half a football field wide, and tall enough to almost reach the nose-bleed section of the football stadium. The total floor space was over 95,000 square feet, and the total volume within the three decks nearly 1.4 million cubic feet. "Naval engineers have discovered that the dimensions and shape of the ark form the most stable ship design known."[7]

It looked nothing like the *Queen Mary* or the *Titanic*. The ark actually resembled a flat-bottomed barge. It wasn't designed to move through the water but simply float on top of it.[8]

This gigantic barge with thousands of built-in compartments was sufficient to carry two of every species [kind] of air-breathing animal in the world.[9] Based on the measurements given and the number of land species cataloged today, not even half of the deck space was needed, which means there was room on the ark for thousands of people. Noah may well have expected many people to come on board and join him in escaping the City of Destruction and the coming wrath of God. Only seven did.

Can you imagine the challenges Noah faced? *Who will believe that water will come down from the sky? Will people really come onto the ark? What do I know about elephants? How will I steer this huge boat? How will all the animals survive inside the ark?*

God had the answers. There is no reference to oars, sails, anchor, captain's wheel, or rudder. God would be in charge of all that. He would do the driving. He was the Captain of this vessel.

Faith Is Demonstrated by Perseverance in the Midst of Mockery

Noah's actions revealed his genuine faith in the word of God. And by his actions, Hebrews tells us, **he condemned the world**.

According to Genesis, Noah spent 120 years building the ark. While doing so, he periodically preached to the crowds who came to see his massive project (see 2 Peter 2:5).

We can only imagine him going up the scaffolding, turning around, and preaching God's message from there. His sermon must have included an invitation and a warning: "Whoever believes this message and enters the ark will be saved from the wrath of God; those who refuse to believe will perish in a coming catastrophe—a flood."

How absurd this all sounded to Noah's generation! Mankind knew nothing about rain, let alone a flood. So people undoubtedly mocked.

"Tell us again. What's that thing you're building?"

"It's an ark."

"What's an ark?"

"Well, I've never seen one before, but according to the blueprints, it's a hollow boat intended to float on water."

"Noah, you're more than a hundred miles from the nearest body of water. Where will the water come from?"

"God will send a flood."

"Oh, and that boat is supposed to float on that flood?"

"That's right."

"Well, okay . . . But why is it so large?"

"It will hold a pair of every kind of land animal that breathes through the nose."

"Oh, and you will round them all up?"

"No, God will bring them to the boat."

"And how will you take care of thousands of animals on a boat?"

"I'm not quite sure."

"And what about us—you know—people? We breathe through the nose too."

"You're invited to join me. There will be plenty of room for many people to come on board."

"What if we don't come?"

"You will drown."

"Who told you that?"

"God did."

"You mean, everybody who doesn't buy your story of a coming flood and get on that boat with you will be killed by the judgment of God?"

"That's right."

The tone of the conversation probably changed near the end. Why? Because Noah was delivering a message of divine judgment to people who wanted nothing to do with God. The thoughts and plans of everyone were entirely given over to evil continually (Genesis 6:5). So, people mocked as Noah pressed on, warning them year after year that judgment was coming.

Try warning your world the same way Noah warned his.

There is another judgment coming. The apostle Peter informs us that the next worldwide cataclysm will be by fire. At the end of human history, God will destroy the earth with fire and then create a new heaven and new earth (2 Peter 3:10-13; Revelation 21:1). Judgment will take place. At that time all who refused to believe the gospel of Jesus Christ will be cast into an eternal lake of fire.

Many react, "You mean to tell me that billions of Muslims, Hindus, and many others will face the judgment of God if they don't believe in your gospel? Is that what you're saying?"

That's not what we're saying; that's what God said. We're just repeating His warning.

It's easy to miss the fact that Noah was a messenger and an agent of rescue. And so is every believer.

It's also easy to miss that everything Noah did was calculated to save people, not condemn them.[10] God's message to unbelievers always has two sides to it: one of rescue and one of judgment.

Noah preached warning and rescue, but nobody beyond his immediate family believed him. Noah doesn't end up in Hebrews 11 because people responded to his voice, but because he faithfully responded to *God's* voice.

Are you willing to persevere in your faith even when surrounded by unbelief, uncertainty, and even mockery? Are you willing to be a lonely man or woman? Do you understand that even though your message is an invitation to salvation and rescue, it is also a message that exposes sin and calls people to admit their guilt?

Alcibiades was a brilliant, yet ungodly, young man living in Athens during the days of Socrates, around four hundred years before the birth of Christ. Alcibiades used to say to Socrates, "Socrates, I hate you, for every time I meet you, you show me what I am."[11]

One of the most upright men who lived in Athens was a man named Aristides. He was even nicknamed "The Just" or "The Righteous One." Eventually, however, the leading citizens and the court of Athens voted to exile him. One man was asked why he voted in favor of exile, and he responded: "Because I am tired of hearing Aristides called 'the just.'"[12] In other words, if he is called "righteous," what does that make me?

Have you ever been called a "goody two-shoes"? That expression came to mind as I thought about the scorn godly people so often suffer. Since I had no idea where the expression came from, I decided to investigate its origin. I found that its roots go back to the children's book *The History of Little Goody Two Shoes*, written in the eighteenth century. The tale is about a little orphan girl who had only one shoe. Out of his kindness, a wealthy man gave her a pair of nice shoes. She was so happy with her new shoes that she told everyone she met, "Two shoes, two shoes!" So, people nicknamed her "Goody Two-Shoes." The gift completely changed her life and made her extremely happy.[13]

As believers, who have received from our adoptive Father the gift of forgiveness, should we not live in such a way that people know our lives have changed? Have you come to terms with the truth that believers are *different*? Are you willing to accept, as A. W. Tozer put it, that "a real Christian is an odd number anyway"? After all, you love someone you have never met, talk every day to someone you cannot see, and expect to go to heaven because of what someone else has done for you.[14]

The danger of a godly life is that it also exposes the ungodliness of those around you. And they will not be happy about the exposure.

During my time in college, I worked on an assembly line making microwaves. The boss moved one of the workers to another position, so I took his job. My job was to take the microwave motor, attach little brackets and a small fan to it, and then hand it to the guy on the assembly line right next to me, as the microwaves moved slowly down the conveyor belt.

The guy I replaced had been able to attach the brackets and fan to the motor just in time for when the next person in the line needed it. Consequently, I was pretty nervous about being able to keep up. But after about an hour—having figured out how to handle everything properly to reposition the stock of fans, brackets, and motors—I found that I was able to make them in plenty of time for the assembly line. In fact, it was so simple that it became boring. I would arrive at my work station and within a couple of hours have plenty of microwave motors stockpiled at my desk. All the guy on the line had to do was reach around and grab one. I was able to go to different places on the assembly line to help out wherever help was needed.

What I didn't know was that the man I had replaced was absolutely infuriated with what I had naïvely exposed. At one point, he came over to me and whispered, "Why are you trying to make me look so bad?"

I was shocked. The thought hadn't crossed my mind.

If you live a life that honors God in every respect, you will expose sin and make waves, sometimes without even knowing it. Are you prepared to ride the waves?

THE GOSPEL ACCORDING TO THE FLOOD

In the narrative of Genesis 6–9, where we read about the ark, the flood, and the remarkable faith of Noah, we also find a few powerful analogies of the gospel of salvation.

The first analogy relates to the *recipient of deliverance*. According to Genesis 6:8, "Noah found favor [grace] in the eyes of the Lord." It was because of God's grace that Noah found his place of safety in the ark and was thus rescued from the wrath of God. Similarly, we also find our place in Christ, saved by His grace alone (Ephesians 2:8-9) and rescued from the coming and eternal wrath of God.

The ark symbolized God's atoning work for mankind. In fact, "the Hebrew word for pitch [Genesis 6:14] . . . has the same root (*kpr*) as that used for atonement" in the sacrificial system later delivered through Moses.[15] In a very real way, then, the word *atonement* first appears in the Bible in relation to Noah's ark.[16] In the ark, mankind would be covered or protected from the wrath of God.

The second analogy relates to the *instrument of deliverance*. The ark was strong enough to handle the waves and the storm that pounded against it and remain safe and afloat for more than a year. Christ is strong enough to carry us safely through the storms of life. He is our ark of safety. No matter how strong the wind or how high the billowing waves, Christ is our strong shelter in the midst of life's storms.

The third analogy relates to the *access to deliverance*. There was only one door into that ark. There was only one way in, only one way to safety as the judgment of God came. There is also only one door that leads to everlasting safety from the wrath of God. Jesus said, "I am the door; if anyone enters through Me, he will be saved" (John 10:9); and, "I am the way, and the truth, and the life; no one comes to the Father but through Me" (John 14:6).

Have you entered through the door of Christ into the ark of salvation by faith in Him alone?

I remember knowing well that I was not saved. I didn't want to give my life to Jesus Christ, but I also knew that I wasn't safe. Having grown up in a Christian home as a missionary kid, I knew enough about the Bible. In fact, I believed the Bible was true, and that's what really scared me.

I knew Christ could come at any moment to rapture His church (1 Thessalonians 4:16-17), so I lived constantly afraid of being left behind as God began to pour out judgment on the earth as promised in the book of Revelation (Revelation 4–19).

I knew I wasn't safe, and I lived in fear. As a teenager, I would get out of bed at night, tiptoe down the hallway, and look in on my little brothers, who shared a room. I would quietly open the door to see if they were still there. After a sigh of relief, I would tiptoe back to my bedroom and try to sleep.

The call to all sinners is this: Enter the ark of Christ and be saved . . . and safe forever. There's still time!

The fourth analogy relates to the *assurance of deliverance*. Inside the ark, there was perfect security. God had shut the door (Genesis 7:16). Neither Noah nor anyone else could open it. Oh, the terror if you were on the outside! But, oh, the security if you were on the inside.

Noah and his family were not only safe; they also were secure. They never needed to fear that God would change His mind and cast them out.

Likewise, the believer in Christ never needs to fear he will lose his spiritual security. Jesus Christ stated, "The one who comes to Me I will certainly not cast out" (John 6:37). In other words, you never need to fear that God will change His mind and throw you overboard.

The fifth analogy relates to the *surprise of deliverance*. Those who entered the ark with Noah emerged to find a newly constructed earth. Likewise, those who are in the ark of Christ will eventually emerge to find a new heaven and new earth (Revelation 21:1).[17]

The final analogy relates to the *triumph of deliverance*. There was no lifeboat hanging from the side of the ark in case passengers needed to abandon ship. Noah and his family didn't bring along life jackets; there were no plastic cards in the seat in front of them with instructions, should the boat go down. There were no emergency portholes. They were safe in the ark of God. It would reach its destination just as God had planned.

Similarly, Jesus Christ, our ark, will succeed in His mission. His gospel will be victorious. The ark of salvation and the church of His redeemed will not capsize. The storms and strategies of hell will not prevail against it. God's church will arrive safely at their eternal destination.

This is the "Gospel according to the Flood." Just as deliverance from the flood came only by means of the ark, so deliverance from the future judgment comes only by means of Jesus Christ. If you have not found refuge in Christ alone yet, there's still time. Flee the destruction now!

If you have believed in the gospel of Jesus Christ, then you are eternally safe. God has called you to a life of faith and faithful obedience. The only qualification Noah possessed was that he walked with God; God would prepare him for everything else.

Answering Objections to the Biblical Flood

It is necessary to address, albeit briefly, five objections to the flood as presented in the Genesis account. While the first three target the flood event itself, the last two target the ark.

Objection #1

The first objection relates to the historicity of the flood—did the biblical flood really happen? One major obstacle to any view that discounts the historicity and authenticity of this event is the statements in other parts of the Bible. For instance, the prophet Isaiah referred to a global flood (Isaiah 54:9); twice Ezekiel mentions Noah specifically as a righteous man (Ezekiel 14:14, 20); Luke includes Noah in the official genealogy of Christ (Luke 3:36); the apostle Peter referred to Noah and the global flood as history (2 Peter 2:5); and Jesus Christ Himself referred to Noah and the flood in His teaching (Matthew 24:37-39). Unless one is also willing to discard these claims in several parts of the Bible, the historicity of Noah and the flood is undeniable.

Another obstacle to those who wish to deny the historicity of the flood is the extrabiblical accounts that depict a cataclysmic event remarkably similar to the biblical flood. Although these accounts are twisted, they still contain kernels of truth. They all testify that some global disaster has obviously taken place. Stories abound among people living in North and South America, Europe, Asia, the Far East, the Middle East, Africa, and the Pacific islands. The depictions tell not only of a flood of water but also of the rescue of a few people.

Native Americans have their legends of a catastrophic flood. One tribe on the west coast tells how one man was saved from a flood by riding on the head of a mythological creature named *Earth*. Another tribe in Arizona talks about a man named Montezuma and a friendly coyote who survived a flood in a boat Montezuma had prepared and kept hidden on a mountain top. After the flood, the coyote was sent out to see how much land was visible.

The natives of Alaska tell the legend of the father of their ancestors, who was warned in a dream that a flood would destroy the earth. So, he built a raft on which he saved himself, his family, and all kinds of animals. The animals could talk in those days, and they soon complained of the long journey. After the waters had gone down, they all alighted from the raft, but the animals lost their powers of speech as a punishment for complaining.

The Hawaiians say that in the old days there was great wickedness on earth and only one man was righteous. His name was Nu-u (sounds a lot like Noah, doesn't it?). Nu-u built a great canoe and filled it with plants and animals and then escaped when a flood came. After the flood ended, he saw the moon for the first time and thought it was a god named Cane. So, he worshipped Cane. But Cane was displeased, and he came down on a rainbow to scold him. Nu-u apologized, and Cane went back up into heaven on the rainbow, but the rainbow remained as a token of Cane's forgiveness.

In Peru, the legend lives on that many years before there were any Incas in the world, all people were drowned by a great flood, except a handful of people who became the forefathers of the now-existing races.

The Cubans tell of an old man who knew a flood was coming, so he built a great ship and brought his family on board along with a host of animals.

A Mexican flood tradition talks about a man who saved himself, his family, and some animals by floating on a raft. As the waters began to subside, he sent out a vulture to find land. The vulture did not return, so he sent out a hummingbird, which did return, carrying a branch with green leaves on it.

The Lithuanians tell how their supreme god decided to destroy everyone by a great flood. After twenty days of raining, only a small group remained high on a mountain. They would have drowned too, but their god accidentally dropped the shell of a nut he was eating and the people used it as a boat and were saved.

The Hindus of India tell of a man who built a ship and, along with seven others, survived a great flood because of a fish that drew the boat to the ground on top of a mountain in the Himalayas. Later, this same man got drunk, and his two sons had to take care of him. Even the ancient Chinese characters that form the word for a large boat are three symbols: one symbol for a person, one symbol for a boat, and another symbol representing eight people inside. There were eight people on that ark centuries ago.[18]

And there are many others. Without any record of Scripture, these stories have been handed down from one generation to another. They communicate this: a global flood occurred on planet Earth.

Objection #2

This worldwide testimony applies also to the second objection, regarding the breadth of the flood. The argument here is that the biblical flood could not have been global. The Bible must be describing a local flood. But look at the biblical account of the flood in Genesis 7:

> Then the flood came upon the earth for forty days, and the water increased and lifted up the ark, so that it rose above the earth. The water prevailed and increased greatly upon the earth, and the ark floated on the surface of the water. The water prevailed more and more upon the earth, so that all the high mountains everywhere under the heavens were covered. The water prevailed fifteen cubits higher, and the mountains were covered. All flesh that moved on the earth perished, birds and cattle and beasts and every swarming thing that

swarms upon the earth, and all mankind; of all that was on the dry land, all in whose nostrils was the breath of the spirit of life, died. (Genesis 7:17-22)

Those who deny the global catastrophe depicted in Scripture and propose a local flood theory face several challenges. First is the biblical language. Moses could not have used any clearer language to describe a global event. Note the repetition of the word *all*, which (surprisingly for some) means *all*. Despite the clear language, many people, even within the church, believe the flood was local, not global. The advocates of the local flood view seek to accommodate modern science, which rejects any idea of a worldwide flood. In the process, they reduce the whole event to a limited disaster that affected only a small segment of the earth and its people. In the minds of many, this makes the flood little more than a folktale created to encourage the people of Israel, as if they needed a good story to pump up morale.

Another obstacle for the local flood theory is the confirmation of other Scriptures. The apostle Peter used the events of Noah and a *global* flood as an illustration of the eschatological *global* firestorm of God's wrath (2 Peter 3:5-7). Most important, Jesus Christ Himself used the flood as a reference to His global judgment yet to come when He returns to earth (Matthew 24:37-39). If the flood was not global, Jesus Christ was wrong and, consequently, the apostle Peter was wrong as well.

The third challenge proponents of the local flood theory face is the character of God. If the flood was only local, God actually becomes a liar. God promised that the flood would never happen again. He even gave the rainbow in the sky as the sign of the covenant promise that He would never flood the planet again (Genesis 9:8-17). But if the flood of Noah was regional, then God was promising there would be no further local floods. This would mean that God has broken His promise to people all around the world over and over again, for local floods continue yearly to bring great damage and loss of life. If the flood of Noah's day was only local, that rainbow in the sky would only be a reminder that God isn't faithful and true after all.

The fourth obstacle for the local flood view is the time it took for the water to drain away. The chronological markers in the flood account make it clear that more than one year passed from the time the flood began until enough land was exposed to permit Noah to leave the ark along with his family and the animals (Genesis 7:11; 8:13-14). Indeed, once the floodwaters reached their peak, it took more than seven months for the waters to recede (7:24–8:3). Such would not have been the case if the flood was local.

The fifth challenge is the preservation of life amid the catastrophe. If the flood was local, animals could have simply migrated to another region, and Noah would not have had to spend over a century building a large boat to rescue the animals. The same applies to the people: they would not have to believe Noah's message and enter the ark in order to be saved but simply move to another region. But the biblical narrative informs us that everyone outside the ark died.

The final obstacle is the earth's wonderful fossil record. It is not only the impressive number of fossils but especially the location in which many are found that gives evidence of a worldwide flood. It is puzzling to the unbelieving scientific community how fossils of sea creatures ended up on the tops of high mountains. As one creationist noted, even at the uppermost parts of Mount Everest, there are fossil layers that have been deposited by water.[19]

Many believing scientists are taking a closer look at the implication of biblical passages like Psalm 104 that indicate that high mountains and deep valleys appeared only after the flood. Indeed, the record from volcanic eruptions and modern-day flooding reveals the astonishing power of natural forces to erode and carve formations out of solid rock.

In one flood, for example, the water and waves tossed 7,000-pound boulders over a breakwater wall and moved 65-ton concrete blocks some 60 feet. And that was just one local flood in Cherbourg, France. Another brief and local flood near Los Angeles, California, "eroded and redeposited up to 100,000 cubic yards of debris from each square mile of the watershed."[20] And still another flood rushed down the Andes in 1970, bringing an avalanche of rocks and mud that buried two entire cities in Peru.[21]

The topography of the earth was completely altered by the global flood. Canyons were carved out by walls of raging water carrying rock, mud, and timber.

The flood not only changed the planet but also "aged" it. What might appear to have required millions of years of erosion could have happened in a single year. The formation of the Grand Canyon, for instance, did not require millions of years of erosion by the Colorado River; it needed only the designing handiwork of a global upheaval as God erupted the fountains of the deep and covered the earth with a massive, raging flood. Unbelieving scientists who ignore the biblical record, however, are led to embrace empty speculations and theories that affirm the earth is millions of years old. Yet at the same time, it is not unusual to find geologists and evolutionists explaining certain discoveries in terms of some kind of cataclysmic event.

When my sons were in second grade, a local professor from one of the nearby universities brought over to their school some fossils and dinosaur bones to discuss the world of millions of years ago. Without my sons knowing, I decided to attend. I wanted to be able to talk to them after class about the theory of evolution.

I stood in the back of the auditorium and listened as the professor remarked near the end of his presentation that the disappearance of dinosaurs has always been something of a mystery, although some disaster may have occurred on the planet to cause their demise. To my amazement, one of my sons raised his hand. I thought, *Oh no, is he falling for this stuff? What's he going to say in front of the entire elementary student body?* With the professor's permission, my son stated, "It was the flood." I was relieved—and proud!

Some unbelievers concede the possibility that a major event happened on the earth that caused massive destruction. The biblical flood certainly was a cataclysmic event, and it explains well the topographical changes the earth underwent and why fossils of marine creatures were buried atop what are today high mountains.

Objection #3

According to evolutionists, dinosaurs and humans never lived during the same period. They argue that dinosaurs had become extinct millions of years before the human species evolved. Therefore, the idea of a global flood, which places dinosaurs and people together just a few thousand years ago, is considered a myth.

Did dinosaurs really live and die out many millions of years ago?

Several years ago, scientists from the University of Montana found Tyrannosaurus rex bones that were not entirely fossilized; there were sections of the bones that were considered fresh. If the bones were millions of years old, the blood cells would have already disintegrated completely. One of these scientists reported:

> The lab was filled with murmurs of excitement, for I had focused on something inside the vessels that none of us had ever noticed before: tiny round objects, translucent red with a dark center—red blood cells! Blood cells are mostly water and could not possibly have been preserved in a 65-million-year-old tyrannosaur. They were indeed hemoglobin fragments.[22]

Little was reported about this incredible find. The implications were simply too enormous to consider.

Objection #4

The fourth objection concerns the millions of insect species—how could they have survived a global flood? For one thing, even if all insects boarded the ark, considering their small size, there would have been ample room. However, according to Genesis 7, only land animals who breathed through nasal passages boarded the ark. Insects do not breathe through nostrils but through tiny pores or tracheae in their exterior skeleton. Outside the ark, they could have survived on mats of vegetation floating on the water, just as they do during regional floods today.[23]

Objection #5

The fifth and final objection involves the survival of the animals inside the ark. If Noah got all 35,000 kinds of land and air-breathing animals on board—and there were at least two of each kind—how did he take care of them all for a year? And how did he manage to get the animals inside the ark in the first place? Those who reject the biblical, global flood see these as insurmountable problems.

One writer recounted the story of a film producer in Italy who "attempted to depict the story of the animals and the Ark. Much time and effort were expended in training a few zoo animals to walk two by two up a ramp into a model of the Ark. When the time came for the filming, however, 'a water buffalo charged up the gangway, crashed through the ark, and headed for Rome at full snort.'"[24]

That's what animals normally do! So how did Noah get the animals into the ark and care for them throughout the year of the flood? Within the biblical interpretive framework and worldview, the answers to these questions rest in the Creator Himself. God acted supernaturally in order to bring the animals to the ark and allow for their care inside the boat.

Genesis 6 informs us that each deck of the ark was to be subdivided into "rooms" (verse 14). The Hebrew word *qēn* can also be translated "nest." In fact, with one possible exception, the term consistently appears in the Old Testament in contexts that refer to birds, either literally or metaphorically, and is translated "nest" (e.g., Numbers 24:21; Deuteronomy 22:6; Psalm 84:3; Isaiah 10:14). This strongly suggests that Noah made nests throughout the ark for the animals in anticipation of them being in a state of inactivity. During this year-long cruise, God may have supernaturally imposed on the animals a year-long hibernation. This would have relieved Noah and his family from the nearly impossible task of feeding and caring for all the animals on a daily basis.

This is certainly a reasonable conclusion, considering what God has done with other animals:

- He changed the mental and vocal capacities of a donkey, allowing it to carry on a conversation with a rather slow prophet (Numbers 22:28).
- He commanded birds to deliver bread to Elijah the prophet (1 Kings 17:6).
- He supernaturally shut the mouths of hungry lions to preserve Daniel alive in the lion's den (Daniel 6:21-22).
- He commissioned a great fish to swallow Jonah and then to lose his appetite three days later (Jonah 1:17; 2:10).
- He had a fish keep a coin in its mouth for Peter to use to pay his taxes (Matthew 17:27).

Another piece of evidence further indicates that the animals acted somewhat differently during that year on the ark: God commanded the animals to breed and multiply *only after* they left the ark (Genesis 8:17). There is every indication that they entered the ark in pairs and left in pairs. Once they were outside the ark, God evidently removed His supernatural restriction over their normal instincts, which would have caused these animals to mate and multiply, had they been awake and fully functioning.[25]

God definitely altered the normal patterns of thousands of animals so that they also left their natural habitat and did something against their natural instincts: they not only walked together in pairs toward an imposing structure but also walked up the gangplank along with other animals they might normally have fought.

God obviously did miraculous things to make the animals arrive, behave around people they did not know, and then take their place in one of thousands of compartments.

⁸*By faith Abraham, when he was called, obeyed by going out to a place which he was to receive for an inheritance; and he went out, not knowing where he was going. ⁹By faith he lived as an alien in the land of promise, as in a foreign land, dwelling in tents with Isaac and Jacob, fellow heirs of the same promise; ¹⁰for he was looking for the city which has foundations, whose architect and builder is God. ¹¹By faith even Sarah herself received ability to conceive, even beyond the proper time of life, since she considered Him faithful who had promised. ¹²Therefore there was born even of one man, and him as good as dead at that, as many descendants* AS THE STARS OF HEAVEN IN NUMBER, AND INNUMERABLE AS THE SAND WHICH IS BY THE SEASHORE. *¹³All these died in faith, without receiving the promises, but having seen them and having welcomed them from a distance, and having confessed that they were strangers and exiles on the earth. ¹⁴For those who say such things make it clear that they are seeking a country of their own. ¹⁵And indeed if they had been thinking of that country from which they went out, they would have had opportunity to return. ¹⁶But as it is, they desire a better country, that is, a heavenly one. Therefore God is not ashamed to be called their God; for He has prepared a city for them. ¹⁷By faith Abraham, when he was tested, offered up Isaac, and he who had received the promises was offering up his only begotten son; ¹⁸it was he to whom it was said, "*IN ISAAC YOUR DESCENDANTS SHALL BE CALLED." *¹⁹He considered that God is able to raise people even from the dead, from which he also received him back as a type. ²⁰By faith Isaac blessed Jacob and Esau, even regarding things to come. ²¹By faith Jacob, as he was dying, blessed each of the sons of Joseph, and worshiped, leaning on the top of his staff. ²²By faith Joseph, when he was dying, made mention of the exodus of the sons of Israel, and gave orders concerning his bones.*

–Hebrews 11:8–22

CHAPTER SIX

WAITING ON THE PROMISES OF GOD

Hebrews 11:8-22

You probably have heard and sung the famous hymn "Standing on the Promises." The lyrics of the first stanza read:

> Standing on the promises of Christ my King,
> Thro' eternal ages let His praises ring;
> Glory in the highest, I will shout and sing,
> Standing on the promises of God.[1]

With one minor change, this hymn summarizes well the lives of Abraham and Sarah:

> **Waiting** on the promises that cannot fail,
> When the howling storms of doubt and fear assail,
> By the living Word of God I shall prevail,
> **Waiting** on the promises of God.

While reflecting on the life of Abraham, the writer of Hebrews condenses into eleven verses several chapters of Old Testament narrative that correspond to more than one hundred years of the patriarch's life. The forefather of our faith is shown in four movements.

HEBREWS 11

THE INITIATION OF FAITH

By faith Abraham, when he was called, obeyed by going out to a place which he was to receive for an inheritance; and he went out, not knowing where he was going. By faith he lived as an alien in the land of promise, as in a foreign land, dwelling in tents with Isaac and Jacob, fellow heirs of the same promise; for he was looking for the city which has foundations, whose architect and builder is God. (Hebrews 11:8-10)

According to the extended account of Abraham's life found in Genesis, he originally lived in the city of Ur, located by the Euphrates River, in what is today southern Iraq.[2] Most people think of the city of Ur as some prehistoric campground, where men ran around with clubs, dragging their wives around by the hair. Archeology, however, has shown that ancient mankind was both sophisticated and educated.

Excavations in Ur of the layer dated to the days of Abraham revealed cobblestone streets, academic buildings, three-story houses with tiled flooring, and buildings with the name *Ur* stamped on their bricks, along with extensive evidence of organization, wealth, and luxury.[3] Archaeologists even found a clay tablet on which someone had written a trigonometry problem, a problem mathematicians at the universities of Oxford and Cambridge were still working on seventy-five years ago.[4]

Archeologists also uncovered at Ur a massive ziggurat, a pyramid-shaped building, from the time of Abraham. At the top of the ziggurat was a room covered in silver and dedicated to their moon-god Nammu.[5] Some historians speculate that Abraham's father was a high priest in this false religion and that their family was one of the most prominent families in the city.

These details help us catch a better glimpse of young Abraham. He was a member of a leading family and lived in an organized, educated, and wealthy city in the Middle East, situated on the bank of a beautiful river. Into that world, the glory of God suddenly appeared to Abraham, immediately shattering the myth of the moon god and revealing the existence of the personal, true, and living God (Acts 7:2).

The Lord's message to Abraham was clear—Abraham was to leave his country, his family, and his world and follow the Lord's leading to another land. Abraham placed his faith in the reality of this living Lord and obeyed the word of God. Abraham's obedience did not *produce* his faith; his obedience *proved* his faith in the living God.

One phrase tucked inside verse 8 is very informative: **And he went out, not knowing where he was going**. There were no billowy clouds spelling out, "Promised Land—800 miles." Abraham had no map, GPS, or favorite restaurants; he had nothing for directions but the command of God's word reiterated in Genesis 12.

Another phrase worth highlighting is found in verse 9, where we're told that Abraham would be **dwelling in tents**. We might be tempted to think, *Well, that's the way they lived back in that primitive society.* Not really. Abraham came from a wealthy family that, more than likely, owned one of those three-story houses with paved floors, open courtyards, luxurious gardens, and a riverfront view. God asked Abraham to leave all that and go live in a tent. That would be similar to God telling you to live the rest of your life in a camper.[6]

Abraham received the promise of land without ever enjoying the possession of the land.[7] And how long would he live like that? For one hundred years. At the end of his life, the only piece of property Abraham actually owned was the grave site he purchased from a pagan in order to bury his wife.

Abraham's theme song would have been, "Waiting on the promises of God."

And for what did he wait? Though we are not told all that God revealed to Abraham, the implications of verse 10 are startling: **For he was looking for the city which has foundations, whose architect and builder is God**. This can only refer to a future city, one Abraham evidently had been told all about. This is "the city of the living God, the heavenly Jerusalem" (Hebrews 12:22). This is the city with gates of pearl and streets of gold. Abraham lived in a tent while waiting for the New Jerusalem, the city designed and built by God.

Oswald Chambers lectured in the Middle East until his sudden death after undergoing an emergency appendectomy from which he never recovered. With his characteristic realism regarding the Christian experience, he wrote, "The life of faith is not so much one of mounting up with wings as eagles, as it is a life of walking and not fainting . . . faith never knows where it is being led, but it loves and knows the One who is leading."[8]

THE CULTIVATION OF FAITH

By faith even Sarah herself received ability to conceive, even beyond the proper time of life, since she considered Him faithful who had promised. Therefore there was born even of one man, and him as good as dead at that, as many descendants AS THE STARS OF HEAVEN IN NUMBER, AND INNUMERABLE AS THE SAND WHICH IS BY THE SEASHORE. (Hebrews 11:11-12)

The second movement of faith the writer of Hebrews describes is the cultivation of faith.

One honest question we might ask is this: Where was Abraham's wife in this walk of faith? In other words, was Sarah frustrated by this change of events? Was she angry about her husband's farfetched plans? What was all this about a promised land, a promised son, and a promised seed? Was Sarah kicking and fussing as she packed her bags and mounted her camel for a long ride to who knows where?[9]

Indeed, she had exchanged her beautiful home by the river for a camper in the wilderness. The writer makes sure we understand Sarah was by Abraham's side. The apostle Peter expands on Sarah's attitude at this point in her life by talking about her submissive spirit (1 Peter 3:6). She too was waiting on the promises of God.

The Genesis account reveals that the great patriarch of faith was originally named Abram. God later changed his name to Abraham. *Abram* means "exalted father" or "father of many." In our modern vernacular, we might say, "Proud papa."

Donald Grey Barnhouse wrote that surely Abram was always having to explain that he was not quite living up to his name. The questions would come from merchants and guests: "Who are you? How old are you? How long have you lived here? What is your name?"

"My name is Abram."

"Oh, congratulations! You must be the proud father of many sons. How many sons do you have?"

"None."

Abram must have steeled himself for the half-concealed snort of sarcastic humor about the absurdity of his name.

Barnhouse writes:

> I once knew a man whose last name was Wrench, who told me how irritating it was to hear the well-worn jokes and wisecracks from people who met him. He would cringe as someone would hear his name and begin one of the wisecracks he had heard before like, "Are you the left-handed wrench; are you related to monkey wrench?" I also know a Mr. Meek who had been asked a thousand times if he had really inherited the earth.[10]

Can you imagine the laughter behind the back of Abram, the "proud father of *many*"?

Abram was willing to wait, until he finally decided he had waited on God long enough. At Sarah's suggestion He had a son with Sarah's servant, Hagar, and they named their son Ishmael.

This was a tragic *lapse* of faith when God wanted to *cultivate* the couple's faith and have them wait for their legitimate son, Isaac, who would continue the promise of God for the coming nation and, ultimately, the Jewish Messiah.

This lapse of faith brought about terrible and longstanding consequences. Ishmael became the father of the Arab nations. To this day, the descendants of Ishmael and the descendants of Isaac are in constant conflict in the Middle East. Every night you can turn on your television to see and hear how the battle is raging. This continuing struggle will end only when Jesus Christ, the Messiah, comes to establish His kingdom with His throne in Jerusalem.

Thirteen years after Ishmael was born, God met with Abram to remind him of the promises and to inform him of a significant name change. The Lord changed his name from Abram ("father of many") to Abraham, meaning "father of multitudes."

This appearance by God tested to the limit the faith of Abraham and Sarah. Both were beyond the ability to conceive naturally; Hebrews 11:12 says of Abraham he was as good as dead. It was simply biologically *impossible* to conceive and deliver the promised son.

It was one thing to call him *Abram* when he had only one illegitimate son; it was audacity to call him *Abraham*, the "father of multitudes." How could God possibly make this come true?

Hudson Taylor, the pioneer missionary in China, put our walk of faith in these terms: "If we are obeying God, the responsibility rests with *Him*, and not with us."[11]

Even when we cannot make it happen, *God* can.

Faith means following God into the unknown—through the tests and trials of life—and then waiting, armed only with the promises of God. The responsibility for fulfilling those promises rests with Him.

The faith of Abraham and Sarah was cultivated while they waited for many years. And even when they failed in their walk of faith, they were given opportunities to learn and grow even more.

THE ANTICIPATION OF FAITH

All these died in faith, without receiving the promises, but having seen them and having welcomed them from a distance, and having confessed that they were strangers and exiles on the earth. For those who say such things make it clear that they are seeking a country of their own. And indeed if they had been thinking of that country from which they went out, they would have had opportunity to return. But as it is, they desire a better country, that is, a heavenly one. Therefore God is not ashamed to be called their God; for He has prepared a city for them. . . . By faith Isaac blessed Jacob and Esau, even regarding things to come. By faith Jacob, as he was dying, blessed each of the sons of Joseph, and worshiped, leaning on the top of his staff. By faith Joseph, when he was dying, made mention of the exodus of the sons of Israel, and gave orders concerning his bones. (Hebrews 11:13-16, 20-22)

The third movement of faith in Hebrews 11 is the anticipation of faith. Abraham and Sarah waited on God's promise of a son for many years. But they also waited for the fulfillment of another promise, as did the other patriarchs. According to verse 16, they were waiting for and desiring **a better country, that is, a heavenly one**, for God **has prepared a city for them**.

All these people died believing the promise was going to happen, though it did not come to pass while they were still alive. Since they waited for a better country, they lived on the earth as **strangers and exiles** (verse 13).

The Greek word for **strangers** (*xenos*) refers to foreigners, who were often viewed with suspicion. It can be translated "refugees."[12] The word for **exiles** (*parepidēmos*) refers to sojourners or pilgrims without permanent residence. The patriarchs lived like refugees in a land they were promised they would inherit. In the meantime, they never were really *home*.

In a letter dated to the second century A.D., Diognetus wrote something striking about the Christians that summarizes well the spirit of the promise we believe by faith: "Every foreign country is their homeland, but every homeland is foreign country."[13]

The same theme of faith was carried on by Abraham's offspring. Hebrews 11:20 tells us, **By faith Isaac blessed Jacob and Esau, even regarding things to come**. We can imagine old Isaac communicating these prophecies and promises to his twin sons.

Jacob followed in the footsteps of his father Isaac and grandfather Abraham, walking on the challenging and yet rewarding ground of faith: **By faith Jacob, as he was dying, blessed each of the sons of Joseph, and worshiped** (verse 21).

The legacy of faith continued as each generation lived out this anticipation of faith: **By faith Joseph, when he was dying, made mention of the exodus of the sons of Israel, and gave orders concerning his bones** (verse 22).

Joseph essentially said, "I've lived here in Egypt just about all my life, but I'm not an Egyptian; I'm an Israelite. So, I don't want my bones placed inside a pyramid, a symbol of idolatry. No. I want my bones to experience the coming resurrection in the land of promise."

These people all died in faith, believing the word of God by faith. Like Abraham and Sarah before them, Isaac, Jacob, and Joseph anticipated the promises of God.

THE DECLARATION OF FAITH

By faith Abraham, when he was tested, offered up Isaac, and he who had received the promises was offering up his only begotten son; it was he to whom it was said, "IN ISAAC YOUR DESCENDANTS SHALL BE CALLED." He considered that God is able to raise people even from the dead, from which he also received him back as a type. (Hebrews 11:17-19)

The fourth and final movement of faith in the life of Abraham is this powerful declaration of his faith, which endured a severe test. God commanded Abraham to offer up his son Isaac as a sacrifice to the Lord. According to God's clear promise, however, Isaac would carry on Abraham's line, ultimately resulting in **as many descendants AS THE STARS OF HEAVEN IN NUMBER, AND INNUMERABLE AS THE SAND WHICH IS BY THE SEASHORE** (Hebrews 11:12). So, the command of God seemed to contradict the promise of God. If Isaac died, the promise would be nullified. Yet God commanded Abraham to give up his son.

This was an irreplaceable sacrifice. By obeying God's command, Abraham put everything on that altar—his hope, his promise, his future, and the object of his love and affection for whom he had waited for decades to hold in his arms. God said in effect, "The son for whom you waited so long and I gave to you—give him back to Me."

I well remember that tiled hallway at Baylor Hospital in Dallas, Texas. I was filling out the paperwork to admit my wife. What began as a routine visit to the doctor turned into immediate admission. Within a few hours, our twin sons would be born.

While Marsha was unexpectedly rushed to the delivery room, the clerk started handing me all these forms to fill out. I had no idea what I was filling out. For all I knew, I had just signed up for five years in the Navy.

At one point, the clerk asked me a rather startling question; "Do you intend to keep your babies after they are born?"

I looked at her and said, "Of course." Then I continued: "Why would you ask me that question?"

She said, "Well . . . we have a list of people who are waiting for parents to give up their infant. If you had filled out this additional form, we would contact the people who are currently at the top of our list."

I wondered aloud, "How many people are on that list?"

She said, "Nearly two thousand couples, and that's just for *this* hospital."

Imagine waiting, waiting, and waiting, until finally you're able to adopt a child. Imagine loving, raising, training that child for several years as he grew. Then, imagine God telling you to give your child away.

What could motivate Abraham to obey God's command to sacrifice Isaac? Verse 19 explains: **He considered that God is able to raise people even from the dead.** Abraham believed that if Isaac died, God could, and would, raise him from the dead. He didn't know *why* God would do it this way, but he trusted that God knew what He was doing.

Abraham did not know Isaac would become a picture, a **type**, of Jesus Christ, God's only Son. Isaac was equally clueless. As much as this was a test of faith for Abraham, it was also a test of Isaac's faith in God's promise that a nation would come through him.

At this point in the narrative, Isaac was not a little boy anymore; he was probably around thirty years old. As a man, Isaac went willingly to the place of sacrifice; he lay upon the wood of that altar of his own volition. Similarly, Jesus Christ, the only unique Son of God, obeyed the will of His Father and was nailed to the cross—the altar of wood—willingly.

The place where Abraham and Isaac passed their test of faith was Moriah, a ridge on which there was a place later known as *Golgotha*. After conquering the whole region, the Romans turned Golgotha into a place of official executions by crucifixion. Golgotha, somewhere on the northern end of Mount Moriah, was where many believe Abraham prepared to offer Isaac. I wouldn't be surprised to learn one day that the very spot where Isaac lay on the altar to die was the exact spot where Christ hung on the cross and gave His life as an offering, by the will of His Father, to pay the penalty for all our sin.

Abraham, the father of faith, along with Isaac, illustrated the depths of the gospel of Christ. Christ would literally die and then literally rise from the dead. Likewise, He will literally come back one day to set up His kingdom in Israel and rule the world. All the faithful will reign with Him on that day.

*****

As sinners redeemed by faith in Jesus Christ, what are *we* waiting for? We are still waiting for these final promises of God to be fulfilled.

In the meantime, we pass our tests of faith as we continue to believe that God will make all things right and give us strength to walk without fainting. Even though circumstances may indicate otherwise, God's promises remain faithful and true.

A generation of Christians have learned "God Will Make a Way," Don Moen's song that affirms God's sovereign involvement in our lives. Most who sing this song, however, are unaware of the tragic circumstances that gave rise to its lyrics.

Late one night, Don received a phone call from his mother-in-law, informing him and his wife of a car accident that would impact their entire family. Don's sister-in-law, her husband, and their four boys were on a trip when they were involved in a car accident. All of them were seriously injured. The nine-year-old son was killed.

As Don and his wife grieved with and for their family members, they felt rather helpless at communicating any kind of hope to the bereaved parents. Don prayed and asked the Lord to help him express hope, perhaps through a song. In a very short time, Don wrote out some lyrics and then composed a tune that to this day gives fellow believers a deep sense of hope in the promises of God.[14] Some of the lyrics are as follows:

God will make a way
Where there seems to be no way.
He works in ways we cannot see;
He will make a way for me.
He will be my guide,
Hold me closely to His side,
With love and strength for each new day;
He will make a way, He will make a way.[15]

The life of Abraham, and others associated with him, challenge us with the truth that faith is walking into the unknown and then waiting.

And then waiting some more . . . all the while clinging to the sufficient, trustworthy promises of God.

²³ By faith Moses, when he was born, was hidden for three months by his parents, because they saw he was a beautiful child; and they were not afraid of the king's edict. ²⁴ By faith Moses, when he had grown up, refused to be called the son of Pharaoh's daughter, ²⁵ choosing rather to endure ill-treatment with the people of God than to enjoy the passing pleasures of sin, ²⁶ considering the reproach of Christ greater riches than the treasures of Egypt; for he was looking to the reward. ²⁷ By faith he left Egypt, not fearing the wrath of the king; for he endured, as seeing Him who is unseen. ²⁸ By faith he kept the Passover and the sprinkling of the blood, so that he who destroyed the firstborn would not touch them.

–Hebrews 11:23–28

CHAPTER SEVEN

FROM RICHES TO RAGS

Hebrews 11:23-28

The history of the automotive industry is a record of personal fortunes, won and lost in the early 1900s.

Among these early automobile entrepreneurs was William Durant. He was the owner of a carriage business in the 1880s, which he built by controlling everything necessary to assemble a buggy. Later, he applied the same process to his "engine-powered buggies" and the industry giant he named General Motors.

In 1905, he rescued from bankruptcy a car maker named David Buick. Durant and Buick formed a partnership and together created an empire by buying out smaller car companies from people like Ransom Olds (of the Oldsmobile) and Walter Chrysler.

Durant also teamed up with a French automaker named Louis Chevrolet. Another Frenchman joined the group who had chosen to name his company after his forefather, Cadillac, the same ancestor who had founded the city of Detroit, Michigan, in 1701.

At one point, Henry Ford agreed to sell his young automotive plant to Durant, but Ford refused stock options in General Motors as payment, insisting on cash instead. They finally agreed on a price, but when Durant missed the closing deadline, Henry Ford changed his mind, which changed the course of automotive history.

Over the next few decades, Durant and his partners made a fortune. In fact, more than seventy men became millionaires by joining or supplying parts to General Motors in the early 1900s.

Notwithstanding his good fortune in the business, Durant would ride a financial roller-coaster, losing, regaining and then losing his fortune again. His last attempt at car making ended in bankruptcy on the eve of the Great Depression.[1]

In 1936, this ingenious creator of a billion-dollar industry was penniless, working as the manager of a bowling alley in Flint, Michigan. Before Durant and his original partner, David Buick, died, they were both too poor to own one of the tens of thousands of automobiles they had actually created.

As tragic as it was, Durant's fall from fame and riches to obscurity and rags is nothing compared to the experience of Moses, our next hero of faith. One of the key differences between Moses and Durant is that Moses walked away from fame and fortune *willingly*.

Hebrews 11 condenses the entire book of Exodus into a few verses in this ledger of faith and presents four chapters in Moses' life. Each chapter begins with the words **by faith** (verses 23, 24, 27, 28).

CHAPTER 1: PRESERVED BY FAITH

By faith Moses, when he was born, was hidden for three months by his parents, because they saw he was a beautiful child; and they were not afraid of the king's edict. (Hebrews 11:23)

As the condensed biography of Moses begins in verse 23, we are immediately struck by the fact that this first chapter of Moses' life is really about the faith of his parents.

Moses was born many years after the death of Joseph. A new pharaoh, who did not know Joseph or care about his legacy in Egypt, adopted a new policy for the Israelites among them: the Israelite race must be enslaved, weakened, and kept from multiplying to the point of becoming a threat to Egyptian rule.

Succeeding kings continued the policy, but the Israelites kept multiplying. Finally, the reigning Pharaoh issued a royal edict ordering the Hebrew midwives to kill any baby boy born to Israelite parents. This plan failed, so

Pharaoh ordered that anyone in the kingdom, irrespective of race, who knew anything about the birth of a Hebrew boy was to throw the baby into the Nile River (cf. Exodus 1:15-22).

Into this hostile environment, an Israelite couple had a baby boy, later named Moses. They already had a daughter, Miriam, and a son, Aaron. The writer of Hebrews tells us that when Moses was born, his parents **saw he was a beautiful child**. This is a somewhat redundant detail to add, don't you think? After all, what parent does not think his or her child is beautiful? Sometimes it's *only* the parents (and the grandparents) who have that opinion!

What are you supposed to say when the proud parents show you their beautiful new baby, who might not impress you as being so beautiful? Years ago I adopted what J. Vernon McGee did when he served in the pastorate. Parents would bring their newborn up to him, and after looking down at the baby and smiling, he would say, "Well now, *that's* a baby!"

Why would the text inform us that Moses was a beautiful child? Of course, he was!

John Calvin was probably right when he wrote that Moses was evidently marked by something out of the ordinary, although we are never told what it was.[2] Josephus, the first-century Jewish historian, speculated a little more. He wrote that Amram, the father of Moses, was visited by God in a vision and informed that his son would be the promised deliverer.

Whatever it was, Amram and Jochebed, the parents of Moses, risked their lives to save their son's life. For three months, they tried to hide him out of sight. How do you hide a newborn and keep him quiet for three months?

Charles Swindoll remembered how his firstborn son never slept through the night for eighteen long, weary months. He writes, "At times I longed for a basket and a Nile River nearby!"[3]

After three months Moses' parents knew they could no longer keep him hidden. Perhaps Pharaoh had begun a house-to-house search for any hidden babies and they knew it was only a matter of time. Rather than giving in or giving up, they hung on **by faith**. Even if it cost their lives, they would not take their son's life.

The book of Exodus informs us that they made a wicker basket and covered it with pitch, or *bitumen*, a type of tar that was used to seal and waterproof the basket. The basket carrying baby Moses was then placed "among the reeds by the bank of the Nile" (Exodus 2:3). It was no accident that they placed the basket in the reeds. Moses' parents undoubtedly knew this was the path where the daughter of Pharaoh walked.

By faith, they placed him there, leaving him in the hands of God to both spare his life and perhaps fulfill the vision they had received of his delivering power.

Exodus 2 further informs us that the daughter of Pharaoh came to bathe at the Nile. The pharaohs had their own bathhouses made of marble, where they did not need to worry about crocodiles. So why would Pharaoh's daughter risk her life by bathing in the Nile? The Egyptians believed the Nile emanated from Osiris, one of their chief gods.[4] The waters were considered divinely empowered, not only to produce long life but *fertility*.

It's possible this Egyptian princess was childless, in which case she probably was not going to the Nile with a bar of soap merely to take a bath and hopefully avoid the crocodiles. She went there to bathe ceremonially with water from the Nile, hoping the mystical waters of the river would help her to have a baby.

God perfectly timed her visit to the Nile to coincide with the presence of a three-month-old baby boy in a floating basket for her to discover. And when she opened the lid of that basket, her heart melted like butter. Though she immediately recognized the child as a Hebrew, the princess was ready to make him her own!

Josephus adds the tradition that the princess took the basket around to several of her maidens to see if one of them could nurse the child, but without any success. Only then did Miriam come out from hiding and ask if she could secure a nurse for the child. The princess agreed and Miriam went and got her mother.[5]

The Bible tells us that the princess paid Moses' mother to raise and care for her own son. And what initiated this wonderful development? An act of preservation, performed **by faith**.

CHAPTER 2:
THE RENUNCIATION BY FAITH

By faith Moses, when he had grown up, refused to be called the son of Pharaoh's daughter, choosing rather to endure ill-treatment with the people of God than to enjoy the passing pleasures of sin, considering the reproach of Christ greater riches than the treasures of Egypt; for he was looking to the reward. (Hebrews 11:24-26)

Exodus informs us that the princess made Moses her legal son and heir (Exodus 2:10).[6] In his sermon recorded in Acts 7, Stephen stated that Moses was educated in all the wisdom of the Egyptians and that he became powerful in speech and action (Acts 7:22).

Just like Joseph before him, on the outside Moses looked and spoke like a member of the Egyptian royal class. But just like Joseph, on the *inside* Moses was a Hebrew believer who worshipped the true God. His mother had taught him well in those early years before he moved into the palace, which most Bible scholars agree would have been around the age of twelve. The faith of his enslaved parents had taken root and become the faith of this young man.

F. B. Meyer, a British pastor and expositor from the 1800s, summarized the wealth and grandeur of Egypt during the days of Moses with the following description:

> What a magnificent land must Egypt have been in those days . . . the banks of the Nile were covered with cities, villages, stately temples and all the evidence of an advanced civilization; whilst mighty pyramids and colossal figures towered to a hundred feet in height. . . .
>
> *The cream of all this was poured into the cup of Moses.* He was brought up in the palace and treated as the grandson of Pharaoh. If he rode forth into the streets, it would be in a princely equipage, amid the cries of "Bow the knee." If he floated on the Nile, it would be in a golden barge, amid the strains of voluptuous music. If he wished for [anything], the

almost illimitable wealth of the treasures of Egypt was within his reach.

When old enough, he was probably sent to be *educated in the college*, which had grown up around the Temple of the Sun, and has been called "the Oxford of Ancient Egypt." There he would learn to read and write the mysterious hieroglyph; there, too, he would be instructed in mathematics, astronomy, and chemistry, in all of which the Egyptians were adept. . . .

But Moses was something more than a royal student, spending his years in cultured refinement and lettered ease. *He was a statesman and a soldier* . . . Josephus writes that whilst he was still in his early manhood the Ethiopians invaded Egypt, routed the army sent against them, and threatened Memphis [the capital]. In the panic the oracles were consulted; and on their recommendation [thirty-year-old] Moses was entrusted with the command of royal troops. He immediately took the field, surprised and defeated the enemy, captured their capital city . . . and returned to Egypt laden with the spoils of victory."[7]

But he soon grew tired of it all. The writer of Hebrews says that Moses **refused to be called the son of Pharaoh's daughter** (Hebrews 11:24).

That Greek verb translated **refused** (*arneomai*) means "to disown" or "to repudiate." It suggests that his refusal was decisive. It was conclusive.[8]

At some decisive moment in time, Moses renounced his royal status and an incredible future. The prince of Egypt walked away from it all! By doing so, he volunteered for one of the greatest riches-to-rags stories ever recorded in human history.

According to verse 25, Moses also refused **to enjoy the passing pleasures of sin**. That is, he renounced all the pomp and ceremony, wealth, and comfort Egypt offered him.

Some super-saint will be quick to say that there are no real pleasures in sin. And it is true that there are no lasting pleasures. But this inspired text reveals there are indeed **pleasures of sin**. And let's be honest. Sin *does* offer pleasures.

The great expositor G. Campbell Morgan wrote nearly a century ago:

> I love this passage because it is so true to life, "pleasures of sin." There are such today. What a stupid thing it is that some people say that there is no pleasure in sin. Of course there are pleasures in sin. Dr. Gordon . . . wrote a hymn, "My Jesus I love Thee." In many books one of the verses reads: "My Jesus, I love Thee, I know Thou art mine / For Thee all the follies of sin I resign." I wonder what made some dear good pious soul alter that. Dr. Gordon did not write that. He wrote: "For Thee all the pleasures of sin I resign." I say some pious soul. . . . Someone thought that it would be wrong to sing about the pleasures of sin.[9]

What motivated Moses to walk away from the pleasures of sin? He compared the pleasures of sin to the reward of Christ, or the pleasure of immortal joys (verse 26). He did not deny that sin offers pleasures; he just knew heaven would offer infinitely superior pleasures.

We often lose heart because we lose sight of the eternal glory that far outweighs our troubles and temptations (cf. 2 Corinthians 4:16-18).

CHAPTER 3: THE SEPARATION OF FAITH

By faith he left Egypt, not fearing the wrath of the king; for he endured, as seeing Him who is unseen. (Hebrews 11:27)

Moses lived 120 years, and his biography can be divided into three sections of forty years each. The first forty years were years of *opulence*, spent in an Egyptian palace. The second forty years were years of *obscurity* in Midian, where he escaped after killing an Egyptian. The final forty years were years of *oversight*, leading the people of Israel.

Because of this easy division, the reader might be tempted to think that verse 27 naturally follows this chronology, detailing Moses' departure from Egypt to live forty years in the desert of Midian. This conclusion is incorrect, however, since we read that Moses left Egypt **by faith . . . not fearing the wrath of the king**.

Exodus 2 informs us that Moses' *first departure* from Egypt was out of fear:

> Then Moses was afraid and said, "Surely the matter has become known." When Pharaoh heard of this matter [that Moses had killed an Egyptian who was beating an Israelite], he tried to kill Moses. But Moses fled from the presence of Pharaoh and settled in the land of Midian, and he sat down by a well. (Exodus 2:14*b*-15)

Clearly then, Hebrews 11:27 must refer to a different event in his life when Moses did not act in fear but **by faith**. That moment will occur forty years later when Moses leads the people of Israel out of Egypt.

While this *second departure* was by faith, it wasn't necessarily easy. What encouraged Moses to stand up to Pharaoh, risk his life and demand the release of the Israelite slaves? The text provides the answer by informing us that Moses **endured, as seeing Him who is unseen**.

To whom does *Him* refer? The answer is found in verse 26: **considering the reproach of *Christ* greater riches than the treasures of Egypt; for he was looking to the reward.** This introduces us to the Person Moses ultimately trusted in: **Christ**, the Messiah.

Moses was unimpressed with the splendor of Egypt because he compared it to the coming kingdom and the city made by God. This revelation was passed on to him from the patriarchs Abraham, Isaac, and Jacob and down through Joseph, whose bones Moses took with him when he left Egypt in the exodus.

To Moses, Egypt was nothing more than a windy sandbar when compared to the coming glorious **reward** of the Messiah's kingdom. With this perspective, he left Egypt by faith, not as a fearful refugee, but as a confident heir to the eternal, Messianic promise.

Kent Hughes wrote:

> I know what would produce such faith in each one of us. Sixty seconds in Heaven. Fifteen seconds to view the face of Christ. . .. Fifteen seconds to survey the angelic host. Fifteen seconds to glimpse Heaven's architecture. And fifteen seconds to behold the face of a loved one now glorified. That is all it

would take. But God is not going to do that for any of us. . ..
I know what else would do it, and that is simply what Moses
did: *believing God's word*. And we can all do that now.[10]

Moses' life was not changed by a sixty-second tour of heaven but by believing God's promise. Likewise, our perspective and focus are changed by faith, by seeing the invisible as reality.

CHAPTER 4: THE INSTITUTION OF FAITH

By faith he kept the Passover and the sprinkling of the blood, so that he who destroyed the firstborn would not touch them. (Hebrews 11:28).

This verse takes us to the eve of the exodus—Israel's departure and freedom from Egyptian bondage. The final plague from God, the death of the firstborn, came riding on the night wind and swept into the land of Egypt to claim the firstborn of every home unguarded by the lamb's blood splattered on the doorposts. For those homes guarded by the blood of the sacrificial lamb, death passed over them (Exodus 12).

Thus, the annual Passover celebration was established—an institution of faith that pointed to the coming Lamb who would be the final sacrifice, permanently ending the power of death and bringing everlasting life. **By faith** Moses kept that first Passover and instituted the ceremony that pointed to the future atonement of Jesus Christ.

The Egyptians were equally interested in life after death. Their religious efforts attempted to appease their gods, doing whatever they could to guarantee a peaceful afterlife. Still, they were never sure they had done enough; not even the pharaohs themselves were convinced.

Religion's favorite word is *do*; Christianity's favorite word is *done*.

This does not mean believers in Christ are exempt from doing good works. We are commanded to perform good deeds (see Titus 3:8). But we do good works not so we *can* be accepted by God, but because we *have* been accepted by Him through faith in Christ. His work of salvation on our behalf is *done*. Our good deeds are thank-you moments for the gifts of God's grace.

*****

Moses gave up everything humanly desirable in this world to gain an eternal reward. Although he was Israel's greatest prophet, lawgiver, historian, and human deliverer,[1] he ended up in an unmarked grave, never entered the land he led millions of people to inherit, and never regained the luxury of a palace or the status of royalty.

Moses becomes our model of faith—the kind of faith that willingly abandons past desires, present delights, and future dreams out of loyalty to God.

Adoniram Judson was the very first Protestant missionary to walk away from a comfortable life in America, spending his life in Burma, just north of Thailand.

Before he embarked on his journey, he fell in love with a wealthy young woman who also loved Christ, as did her parents. Adoniram wrote a letter to her father, asking permission to marry his daughter. His letter realistically revealed the cost of serving Christ in Burma and his proposal spelled out the sacrifice it would demand of both his wife *and* her parents:

> I have now to ask whether you can consent to part with your daughter early next spring, to see her no more in this world? Whether you can consent to her departure to a heathen land, and her subjection to the hardships and sufferings of a missionary life? Whether you can consent to her exposure to the dangers of the ocean; to the fatal influence of the southern climate of India; to every kind of want and distress; to degradation, insult, persecution, and perhaps a violent death? Can you consent to all this, for the sake of Him who left his heavenly home and died for her and for you; for the sake of Zion and the glory of God? Can you consent to all this, in hope of soon meeting your daughter in the world of glory, with a crown of righteousness brightened by the acclamations of praise which shall resound to her Savior from heathens saved, through her means, from eternal woe and despair?[12]

Her father said *yes*, and so did she!

God's plans may call us to give up, wait for, pursue, begin, or renounce many things for His name's sake. The only way we can possibly do any of it is by faith.

Again, faith is abandoning past desires, present delights, and future dreams out of loyalty to God in light of our future with God that will compensate us beyond our wildest imagination.

In the meantime, we live in a manner that declares, "Goodbye Egypt . . . we're on our way to the Promised Land."

²⁹By faith they passed through the Red Sea as though they were passing through dry land; and the Egyptians, when they attempted it, were drowned. ³⁰By faith the walls of Jericho fell down after they had been encircled for seven days. ³¹By faith Rahab the harlot did not perish along with those who were disobedient, after she had welcomed the spies in peace.

–Hebrews 11:29–31

CHAPTER EIGHT

FAITH FROM THE UNLIKELY

Hebrews 11:29-31

A reporter once asked Walt Disney how it felt to be a celebrity. He responded:

> As far as I can remember, being a celebrity has never helped me make a good picture, or a good shot in a polo game, or command the obedience of my daughter, or impress my wife. It doesn't even seem to help keep fleas off our dogs, and if being a celebrity won't give me an advantage over a couple of fleas, then I guess there can't be that much in being a celebrity after all.[1]

The average person on the street is somewhat convinced that famous people just feel better, enjoy better lives, and have a leading edge on happiness, perspective, and practical wisdom.

Unfortunately, many Christians are convinced that God's kingdom is enhanced by famous people—individuals with natural charisma, special talents, and a stellar track record. The church seems overly excited when well-connected people come to faith in Christ. Surely the angels sing a little louder at *their* conversion! We're not surprised at all to find famous men and women included in Hebrews 11. But we *are* surprised when God includes some rather ordinary people in this legacy of faith, people as well known for their failures as for their successes. God is evidently interested in redefining true, heroic faith as He adds to this inspired list.

THREE PRINCIPLES OF FAITH
Faith Is Willingness to Obey God Even When It Seems Hopeless

By faith they passed through the Red Sea as though they were passing through dry land; and the Egyptians, when they attempted it, were drowned. (Hebrews 11:29)

The historical context that makes verse 29 stand out is that when the Israelites left Egypt, everything went well until they heard the rumbling of Pharaoh's army. They quickly found themselves trapped between the Red Sea in front of them and Pharaoh's soldiers approaching from behind.

Critics are quick to point out that in the Old Testament **Red Sea** can be translated "Sea of Reeds," and they conclude this is some shallow, knee-deep swampland. Wading across it would require no miracle. If that were true, how embarrassing for the entire Egyptian army to drown in knee-deep water.

Contrary to the liberal opinion, **the Red Sea** was deep enough for the children of Israel to believe they were stuck, hopelessly trapped with no way out!

In light of their obvious predicament, they cried to Moses:

> Is it because there were no graves in Egypt that you have taken us away to die in the wilderness? Why have you dealt with us in this way, bringing us out of Egypt? Is this not the word that we spoke to you in Egypt, saying, 'Leave us alone that we may serve the Egyptians'? For it would have been better for us to serve the Egyptians than to die in the wilderness." (Exodus 14:11-12).

To people consumed with *fear*, Moses issued a command that transformed them into people of *faith*:

> But Moses said to the people, "Do not fear! Stand by and see the salvation of the LORD which He will accomplish for you

today; for the Egyptians whom you have seen today, you will never see them again forever. The LORD will fight for you while you keep silent." (Exodus 14:13-14)

God asked them to exercise faith by doing the one thing they could do—remain quiet.

According to the full account in Exodus, God caused an east wind to sweep in, thus dividing the waters of the sea in two (Exodus 14:21). The powerful wind dried out the seabed so that in a few hours some three million Israelites by faith walked between two walls of water.

At this point, you might have a mental picture of Moses with long white hair and beard billowing in the wind as he leads the Israelites through this narrow passage in the sea. You might picture a long line of people following, side by side, two or three abreast.

Consider a more realistic picture of what would be required to enable millions of people to travel across a dry seabed in a single night. Expositors (with calculators) estimate that the path through the sea would have needed to be a mile wide. And the line of people, wagons, and cattle could have stretched for nearly a mile as well.

Exodus records that the waters stood up like a wall (Exodus 14:22). In the next chapter, we are told in poetic form that the waters "congealed" (15:8); that is, they were thickened to become "like solid masses."[2] Even the form of the water was part of the miracle.

The Israelites **passed through the Red Sea** . . . and that took faith.

In his commentary on this passage, Arthur Pink wrote there are three degrees of faith. First is the faith that *receives*. Like beggars, we receive Christ. There is the faith that *reckons*, that counts upon God to fulfill His promise whether we do anything or not. And third is the faith that *risks*. This faith believes God's promises and also dares to do something for the Lord.[3]

The faith that risks is exemplified by David, who ran out to meet Goliath; by the prophet Elijah, who challenged the false prophets on the top of Mount Carmel; and by the apostles, who defied the Jewish leaders and continued to preach the gospel of Christ.

And this was the faith of the Israelites, as well. They could not just believe and receive the promise. They had to risk everything, walk down the banks of the Red Sea and through that dry seabed between towering walls of water that could come crashing down on them at any moment.

Passing through the sea was one of the greatest corporate acts of faith in Israel's history. They risked their lives without any guarantee other than the promise of God.

Hebrews 11 informs us that the Egyptians went in after the Israelites. God began to trouble and confuse them. The Egyptians' chariot wheels began to fail, and then the two walls of water collapsed upon them with a crushing, fatal force (Exodus 14:23-28).

Faith Is Willingness to Follow God Even When It Seems Ridiculous

By faith the walls of Jericho fell down after they had been encircled for seven days. (Hebrews 11:30)

There is a forty-year gap between verses 29 and 30. The Israelites who crossed the Red Sea were not the same Israelites who crossed the Jordan and conquered the city of Jericho, an event that took place a generation later and is narrated in detail in the book of Joshua.

Similar to the Red Sea miracle, God miraculously cut off the flow of the Jordan River upstream, and the people walked across on dry land. Unlike after the crossing of the Red Sea, however, this time they trusted God to lead them on their way as they moved into the promised land.

Their first stop was the walled fortress of Jericho. Jericho was a massive fortress standing in their way, and well-equipped, heavily-armed legionnaires stood ready to defend it.[4]

Decades earlier, while the Israelites were still in the wilderness, spies were sent into Canaan. They saw fortified cities like Jericho and reported back, "The people are bigger and taller than we; the cities are large and fortified to heaven" (Deuteronomy 1:28). This report had thrown Israel into such panic that they spent the next thirty-eight years wandering in the desert because of their unbelief in God's promise and power. Only two of the twelve spies sent into the land had insisted the Israelites could take it, but they were outvoted.

Those two spies—Joshua and Caleb—now much older, were back, ready to lead and complete the conquest of the land. And what was the military plan for conquering Jericho?

Once a day for six days, soldiers, priests, and the people were to walk around the city of Jericho. Priests were to carry the ark of the covenant, and seven of them were to continually blow their ram's horns. Then, on the seventh day, they were to walk around the city seven times. Then, after a long trumpet blast, the people were to shout at the top of their lungs, and the walls would fall down (Joshua 6:1-6). This was the plan God gave them. Was there a Plan B?

Imagine some Canaanite soldiers on top of the city walls looking down at this procession and yelling to some Israelites: "What in the world are you doing?"

"We're conquering your city."

"How is that?"

"We're going to walk around your city once a day for six days."

"That's pretty scary! Then what?"

"Then we're going to walk around it seven times on the seventh day."

"That's terrifying! Then what?"

"Then our head priests are going to play a long note on their trumpets, and we're going to yell at your city at the top of our lungs."

"Horrors! Then what?"

"Then the walls are going to come crashing down."

This conversation, of course, never happened because part of God's command was that all the people remain absolutely silent during their march around the city. One can only imagine the potential grumbling after the fourth day: "Hey, not one stone has even budged . . . we ought to be building ladders or digging tunnels!"

"How much mischief is wrought by people perpetually talking of the *difficulties* in the task confronting us. All real Christian work is beset with difficulties—Satan will see to that."[5]

Hudson Taylor, the missionary pioneer to China, said that there are three stages to God's will: impossible, difficult, and done.[6] There will always be difficulties, challenges, and disappointments. We are tasked with reaching fallen sinners, yet we ourselves, while redeemed, are imperfect people who still sin. How tough can that be?

Opportunity usually arrives with an equal amount of opposition. And the greater the opportunity, the greater the opposition seems to be.

As Adoniram Judson baptized a respectable merchant in Burma, a huge crowd showed up and lined the river. As soon as the man came up out of the water, the crowd began to laugh.[7] *What a fool! What a crazy ordinance!* they must have thought. When someone is baptized today, we celebrate. Imagine following God's command and being mocked because of your obedience.

The pagan soldiers up on the wall no doubt laughed and jeered while the Israelites continued their walk around the city. After the thirteenth time, in obedience to God's command, the priests blew that long note, and all the people shouted. Perhaps, even to *their* amazement, the walls came tumbling down.

Impossible . . . difficult . . . *done*!

Faith Is Willingness to Forget the Failure of the Past and Risk Everything about the Future

By faith Rahab the harlot did not perish along with those who were disobedient, after she had welcomed the spies in peace. (Hebrews 11:31)

Tucked into this amazing moment of national faith is a vignette of personal faith, along with a surprising entry in this catalog of faith: **By faith Rahab the harlot.**

Rahab was famous, though for all the wrong reasons. She certainly had connections, though they were all the wrong ones. Rahab is probably the last person we would expect to be converted to faith in the God of Israel.

She welcomed the spies who came to her secretly and confessed, "We have heard how the LORD dried up the water of the Red Sea before you when you came out of Egypt" (Joshua 2:10). Since the Israelites had only recently crossed the Jordan River, she may not have heard the news of that miracle. But she *had* heard how they had crossed the Red Sea forty years earlier and defeated the Amorite kings east of the Jordan more recently. She admitted,

"Our hearts melted and no courage remained in any man any longer" (verse 11).

Years earlier, when the spies returned and said there were giants in the land and cities with walls reaching up to heaven, the Israelites' hearts had melted in fear. But now Rahab reveals that the hearts of these pagan kingdoms had shook with fear. All this time, they had been terrified of the Israelites' God.

A prostitute's faith had been greater than an entire generation of Israelites. This is clear from her profession of faith to the spies: "I know that the LORD has given you the land" (Joshua 2:9); "The LORD your God, He is God in heaven above and on earth beneath" (verse 11).

Rahab was essentially requesting, "Can I join you? Would your God accept someone like me?" And the answer was yes. Rahab became the first convert in the promised land.

Some have tried to soften the edges of this story by saying that the Hebrew word for "harlot" (*zonah*) in Joshua 2:1 can be translated "innkeeper," since the two often were part of the same industry. The problem with this suggestion is that the Septuagint, the Greek translation of the Hebrew Bible translated before the time of Christ, used the Greek word *pornē*, which clearly means prostitute.[8] More important, both Hebrews 11:31 and James 2:25 use the word *pornē* to describe Rahab. Rahab did not manage a bed and breakfast . . . she ran a brothel.

Why soften the edges? This is precisely the point of her conversion: God demonstrated His grace to an unlikely prospect who then became a living testimony of faith in God. She staked her entire future on the grace of God.

TWO ENDURING TRUTHS

These narratives of surprising faith point out two enduring truths.

Your Weakness Does Not Hamper God's Performance

In his commentary on Hebrews 11, Griffith Thomas writes, "Someone has said that the believer, like David of old, has five pebbles available for use: God is, God has, God does, God can, God will."[9]

Little pebbles work really well in the hands of little people of faith. God can make giants fall, waters part, walls collapse, and sinners repent. Humble people of faith give all the credit to God.

A church leader once said to Hudson Taylor, "You must often be conscious of the wonderful way God has prospered the [China Inland Mission]. I doubt if any man living has had a greater honor." He responded, "I sometimes think that God must have been looking for someone small enough for Him to use, so that all the glory might be His, and that He found me."[10]

We should all talk like that.

Your Past Does Not Hinder God's Plans

It is unlikely that your past is more tainted than Rahab's. Follow her example, and leave your reputation in the hands of God, and go about your business of living for Him.

And don't overlook Rahab's *future*. She and her family were rescued after the walls of Jericho fell. It wasn't long before a godly Israelite man named Salmon met her. He must have been moved by her faith and genuine conversion, demonstrated by what she had risked. The two married—Rahab the former harlot and Salmon, a prince of Judah in the royal, messianic line.

This couple had a baby boy, and they named him Boaz. Boaz surely grew up hearing the testimony of his mother's faith; her past didn't ruin his life either. He grew up observing his faithful Israelite father and his faithful Canaanite mother. Eventually, Boaz married a Moabite woman named Ruth, who, like Boaz's mother, left her past nation of idolaters behind and put her faith in the God of Israel. A few generations later, their great-great-grandson was born. His name was David (Matthew 1:5-6).

Take note of Rahab's past, but don't overlook her future!

Some time ago, I preached in Medellin, Colombia. The auditorium was packed an hour before the service began. At the end of the service, an invitation was given for those who wanted help and counsel. Many people made their way to the front to talk to the leadership. About an hour later as the building was nearly empty, a staff member brought a woman up on stage. It was evident that many had been praying for her, and she had come to that special event. With the help of a translator, this woman told me she was going to leave her life as a prostitute and drug courier for one of the cartels. Tears of joy filled her eyes as she told me that she now belonged to Jesus Christ.

Every one of us has the same intersection with God's grace. For Christ came, the offspring of mixed Gentile and Jewish blood, to redeem for Himself a bride from every tongue, tribe, and nation.

Believer, take note of your past . . . just imagine your future!

³²And what more shall I say? For time will fail me if I tell of Gideon, Barak, Samson, Jephthah, of David and Samuel and the prophets, ³³who by faith conquered kingdoms, performed acts of righteousness, obtained promises, shut the mouths of lions, ³⁴quenched the power of fire, escaped the edge of the sword, from weakness were made strong, became mighty in war, put foreign armies to flight. ³⁵Women received back their dead by resurrection.

–Hebrews 11:32–35*a*

CHAPTER NINE

AN ANCIENT MEMORIAL

Hebrews 11:32-35a

On November 13, 1982, Americans paused to pay tribute to fallen service members who gave their lives during the Vietnam War. On that day, "The Wall," as it has since been nicknamed, was dedicated in Washington, D.C.

Made out of black granite and standing ten feet tall at its highest point, the wall stretches some five hundred feet. Carved into the granite panels are the names of the fallen.

Beyond a brief inscription at the top honoring those listed on the wall, nothing more is said. Row after row simply displays the names of those who died in the war.[1]

When the monument was dedicated, there was an outcry of public disapproval. Many argued that there should be famous quotes embedded into the monument, maybe pictures, carvings, or tributes to the dead. There should be something more! But over time, the profound message sunk in. Anything said would be insufficient. The 58,000 names silently bear witness to their ultimate sacrifice in life and in death.

In November of 1863, Americans were grieving the losses from another war—the Civil War. Out on a field where a recent battle had taken the lives of thousands of soldiers, Abraham Lincoln stood on a platform and delivered a two-minute speech. His brevity was shocking. When he sat down, a member of the Philadelphia press corps whispered to him, "Is that all?" He replied, "That is all."

The newspapers scoffed at such a failed performance. According to the *Chicago Times*, every American would be ashamed at the president's silly and diluted words; society at large considered his remarks crude and insufficient. After all, the speaker who preceded Lincoln had spoken for more than an hour. The majority of newspapers never even put Lincoln's speech on the front page.[2]

Lincoln's Gettysburg Address *was* brief, but soon everyone discovered its depth. It is now considered one of the greatest American speeches ever delivered and has become a national treasure.

You don't need a lot of words to describe truly great events and truly courageous people. Like an ancient memorial, the writer of Hebrews lists the names of heroes of the faith beginning at verse 32. Then, in verses 33 to 35, he briefly reviews some accomplishments of faith in less than sixty words.

SIX MEN AND SOME PROPHETS

And what more shall I say? For time will fail me if I tell of Gideon, Barak, Samson, Jephthah, of David and Samuel and the prophets. (Hebrews 11:32)

The author begins verse 32 by writing, **What more shall I say?** In other words, "What more do I need to say? Faith is fully trusting God for what He has promised, regardless of outward circumstances."

He then adds the statement, **For time will fail me**, or, "I don't have enough time to give all the illustrations of genuine faith."

While this inspired author struggles with a lack of time and space to record everyone, his list is surprising for a number of reasons.

First, the names are not listed in chronological order. This detail is a wonderful evidence of the inspiration of Scripture through the personality of a human author. Someone editing these comments later would have put the names in order. Barak served *before* Gideon, and Samson came *after* Jephthah. The author just seemed to name them as they came to his mind.

Second, names you might expect to be mentioned are left out and surprising names are included.[3] We can understand David and Samuel. But Gideon? Barak? Samson? Why not Nehemiah, Jeremiah, Isaiah, Hezekiah,

Josiah, Hannah, or Ruth? If you're going to simply list some names, at least pick some that had better reputations.

But that's the point. They didn't have polished resumes and clean rap sheets. For the most part, they were far from perfect. But they were *available* for God to use.

Gideon: Faith Versus Fear

The first character mentioned in Hebrews 11:32 is **Gideon**. The full account of this judge is found in Judges 6–8.

Originally, Gideon wasn't exactly a hero of the faith. He was so afraid of the Midianites that he hid in a winepress. Even after the Lord spoke to him, he was so certain that God had chosen the wrong man to be a judge that he decided to perform the famous "fleece test." He put a fleece of lamb's wool out in the yard and declared that in the morning if the fleece was wet with dew and the ground around it was dry, he would be sure the Lord would deliver Israel through him. The next morning, Gideon wrung out a bowl full of water from the fleece, and the ground was dry.

Not convinced, he decided to perform the same test with different conditions: this time the fleece must remain dry while the ground around was wet. And that's exactly what happened.

Reluctantly, Gideon pulled together an army of 32,000 men, but when God said these were too many soldiers, his army was reduced to 10,000.

God insisted Gideon's army was still too large. To paraphrase His instructions, He said, "Take the men to the water and let them get a drink. Dismiss all those who kneel down and drink directly from the spring but keep those soldiers who kneel down and collect the water in their hands, raising it to their mouths." In other words, keep only the soldiers who remain alert for enemy attack.

Of those 10,000 soldiers, 9,700 of them dropped down on all fours and started drinking directly from the spring. I can imagine Gideon shouting: "No! Use your hands!"

In the end, though, only 300 men were left with Gideon. The Midianite army he was facing numbered 135,000, all well-armed, professional soldiers.

Instead of running to the nearest winepress to hide, this farmer turned courageous judge and did not run. When God revealed His peculiar battle strategy of broken clay pitchers, torches, and trumpets, Gideon obeyed and won a great victory.

Here's the lesson: Gideon demonstrated faith that overruled personal fear.

Barak: Faith Versus Pride

Judges 4–5 presents the full narrative of the judge **Barak**. Barak was called by God to lead the Israelite troops into battle against Sisera, who commanded the Canaanite chariot army of King Jabin. Nothing would have thrilled Barak more than to defeat Sisera, and God even promised ahead of time that he would be victorious.

Some believe Barak was hiding out in a city of refuge when God called him to become a judge. God's promotion would bring Barak incredible fame as a victorious judge and general. But God's plan also was to turn Sisera's name into an embarrassment for every enemy nation. In order to do that, He would not allow Barak to kill him. A woman would take Sisera's life. Barak swallowed his pride and submitted to God's plan, which would bring God all the glory.

Harry Truman once said, "It is amazing what you can accomplish if you do not care who gets the credit."

Here's the lesson: Barak demonstrated faith that overpowered his personal pride.

Samson: Faith Versus Failure

Judges 13–16 tells the full story of **Samson**, a man who really should have learned that little children's chorus about being careful what your eyes see. It would have saved him much trouble and kept him from that fateful haircut.

His eyes fell on Delilah, and she coaxed out of him the secret of his great strength. Though his hair did not give him power, it represented his commitment to the Lord to obey the restrictions of the Nazirite vow.

Samson let down his guard. While he slept with his head on Delilah's knees, she called for a Philistine man to come and cut off his hair. Moments later Samson awoke to realize his vow to God was broken and his strength was gone. The Philistines put out his eyes and put him into prison.

Samson's last act, however, was his greatest.[4] He called upon God for strength and pushed over two support columns in the Philistine temple of Dagon. The temple came crashing down, and though Samson was crushed as well, his final act killed more Philistines than he had killed previously his entire life.

Failure is never final.

Here's the lesson: Samson demonstrated faith in God that overcame past failure.

Jephthah: Faith Versus Personal Heritage

The record of **Jephthah** appears in Judges 11. He was driven away by his own half brothers because he was the illegitimate child of a prostitute. He lived on the east side of the Jordan where he led a notorious gang of undesirables. When God's surprising search for a courageous hero bypassed everyone else and found him, Jephthah accepted the call of God and led the Israelites to victory over the Ammonites.

For anyone wondering if God wants only people with a respectable family pedigree, Jephthah becomes God's visual aid that He will use anyone who is available and willing to obediently follow Him in faith.

Here's the lesson: Jephthah demonstrated faith in God that overcame his personal heritage.

David: Faith Versus the Impossible

The heroic acts of **David**, demonstrating faith in God, began while he was still tending sheep. He risked his life to defend the reputation of God against a giant named Goliath and an army of Philistines. First Samuel 17 provides the narrative of that death-defying act of faith.

Keep in mind that young David wasn't interested in making a name for himself by an act of bravery. I've read brief biographies of individuals who attempted to survive plunges over Niagara Falls to win fame and fortune. Most did not succeed.

In 1901 Annie Taylor, a retired schoolteacher, went over the falls as a publicity stunt. She was sixty-three years old, though she claimed to be only forty-three. She devised a modified pickle barrel, cushioned inside with pillows. On her birthday, October 24, she climbed into the barrel and went over the falls holding her cat. Fortunately, she survived. Upon being pulled out, she said, "No one ought ever to do that again."

But in 1930, George Stathakis did. He got into an even heavier barrel and went over the falls with his pet turtle inside, along for the ride. Only the turtle survived.

Jessie Sharp went over the falls in 1990 in a closed-deck canoe. He was an expert kayaker and was convinced that Niagara Falls, considered a class 6 rapids, could be conquered. In fact, he was so confident that he even refused to wear a helmet. He explained that a helmet would obscure his face from the cameras he knew would be waiting for him later. He never surfaced and his body was never found.[5]

What a tragic, trivial cause on which to risk one's life.

If you had been on the side of that hill with the Israelite army and saw a young shepherd boy run into that valley toward a giant named Goliath, you would have thought the same thing about David: "What a waste of life."

But this wasn't an act. There were no cameras around. David wasn't trying to become famous. He was concerned about the fame of God. He exercised faith in the name of the Lord, and his victory became a lasting illustration of faith in the face of the impossible.

Here's the lesson: David demonstrated faith in God that overwhelmed personal impossibilities.

Samuel and the Prophets: Faith Versus External Pressure

The list ends with **Samuel and the prophets**. Their testimony is recorded throughout much of the Old Testament. It is possible to define their faith categorically as a faith that overcame pressure to compromise with their surrounding culture.

A prophet was a different kind of warrior. Prophets preached and confronted, not their enemies, but their families. They spoke to their own people. It takes as much courage to stand for Christ in front of family and coworkers as strangers and enemies.

For the most part, the prophets stood before their fellow Israelites and simply declared, "Thus says the Lord." Great was the pressure upon them, from both the leadership and the masses, to lay aside God's oracle and

AN ANCIENT MEMORIAL

embrace the people's sinful lifestyle. Their persistence in proclaiming the Lord's message cost some of them their lives.

Here's the lesson: The prophets demonstrated faith in God that overcame the pressure to conform.

NINE FRUITS OF FAITH

Who by faith conquered kingdoms, performed acts of righteousness, obtained promises, shut the mouths of lions, quenched the power of fire, escaped the edge of the sword, from weakness were made strong, became mighty in war, put foreign armies to flight. Women received back their dead by resurrection. (Hebrews 11:33-35a)

In these verses, the writer of Hebrews delivers in short sentence fragments the history of Israel. These are reminders of the power of faith revealed in and through people, or what one author called the *fruits* of faith.[6]

- **Conquered kingdoms:** This might be a reference to Joshua, who defeated the enemy kingdoms in the promised land, or even to David who later defeated the Philistines.[7]

- **Performed acts of righteousness:** The author may have had in mind the prophet Daniel, who maintained his integrity for seventy-five years as he served several pagan kings.

- **Obtained promises:** Performing acts of righteousness is faith *living* biblically; obtaining the promises is faith *waiting* biblically. One author described these two ideas as faith behaving and faith believing.[8] Our greatest step of faith is usually the next one, no matter what that is.

- **Shut the mouths of lions:** In all likelihood, this phrase refers to God's miraculous protection of Daniel in the lions' den. While we might not be thrown to lions, we must not overlook the fact that the devil is on the hunt: he "prowls around like a roaring lion, seeking someone to devour [i.e., discredit]" (1 Peter 5:8). Every time you trust God, do the right thing, and respond biblically, thus avoiding the snare of temptation, you effectively shut the mouth of that old lion.

- **Quenched the power of fire:** The quenching of fire might be a reference to Daniel's three friends who were thrown into the fire by the Babylonian king, Nebuchadnezzar, only to come out unscathed and unharmed. Paul informs us that our faith is the shield whereby we protect our lives from the flaming arrows of the Evil One—fiery darts he has dipped in temptation, impatience, unbelief, or pain (Ephesians 6:16). We might not be thrown into a fiery furnace or into a den of lions, but every day, whether we realize it or not, we face the threat of a firefight and a cunning lion. We cannot face either one without faith.

- **Escaped the edge of the sword:** In 1 Samuel 18 and Jeremiah 39, servants of the Lord escaped from certain death by the sword through the supernatural assistance of God.

- **From weakness were made strong:** This statement could be applied to Gideon, David, and others in the Old Testament. One of the benefits of growing older in the faith is that you discover just how weak you are. Rather than growing more independent, the person of faith grows more dependent and comes to understand what Christ meant when He told His disciples: "Apart from Me you can do nothing" (John 15:5).

- **Became mighty in war, put foreign armies to flight:** Many Old Testament figures fit this description, including Abraham, Gideon, Joshua, and Jonathan.

- **Women received back their dead by resurrection:** The widow of Zarephath's son was raised to life by Elijah (1 Kings 17:17-24), and the Shunammite's son was raised by Elisha (2 Kings 4:18-37).

FINAL OBSERVATIONS FROM THIS MEMORIAL TO FAITH

Most Demonstrations of Faith Come through Surprised People

The individuals mentioned in these verses put their lives on the line and acted in faith. But we should not think Gideon marched up the hill to battle the Midianites, thinking, *Ah! The torch-and-the-trumpet strategy. This works every time!*

Acts of faith take place when there is no question about who must perform the mighty deed—it must be *God*.

May God grant us lives and ministries that can be explained only in terms of God's power accomplishing His work through available people of faith.

Some Demonstrations of Faith Come through Hesitant People

The people God chooses to use often are fearful people. They are the ones who hesitate to raise their hand and step forward. Yet God delights in teaching the hesitant how to act in faith, trusting Him to accomplish His purposes through them.

Some Demonstrations of Faith Come from Inexperienced People

Such was the case with Jephthah, Josiah, Esther, Ruth, and many others. Faith doesn't demand past experience; it delights in a personal response.

Every Demonstration of Faith Comes through Imperfect People

If you study carefully the lives of these Old Testament saints, every one of them had a flawed faith:

- Gideon failed to maintain a humble walk of faith.
- Barak failed to fully trust the Lord in faith.
- Jephthah foolishly boasted in his faith.
- Samson repeatedly lapsed in his faith.
- David failed to consistently lead in faith.

Like the original readers of Hebrews 11, we can identify with this list of Old Testament saints. It includes those who were *not* consistently strong or brave. While they were not always faithful, God was.

One of my favorite heroes of the faith lived through several challenges to his young faith as he prepared for missionary service.[9]

Hudson Taylor wrote extensively to his sister. In his letters, he wrote that he had decided to prepare for the mission field by living off the smallest amount of money and food possible. He moved into the slums of London, even though he was apprenticed to a medical doctor as he prepared for his own license. He found that he could live off porridge and bread most of the week, eating meat only occasionally. He used all his remaining money for medical supplies as he personally assisted the poverty-stricken people in his neighborhood.

Hudson had a problem, though: the medical doctor for whom he worked often forgot to pay his weekly salary. Hudson had to remind him every week, and it became so frustrating to Hudson that he finally decided to give it over to the Lord and trust the Lord to remind the doctor to pay him. He felt this would be a good way to develop faith to simply trust the Lord.

After he made that pact with the Lord, however, the doctor did not pay him again.

God didn't seem to be reminding the boss. Eventually, the rent was due, and Hudson had no money to pay; his food was running out as well.

On a Friday, near closing time at the clinic, the doctor, again with no clue that he owed Taylor another week's salary, suddenly turned to him and said: "By the [way], Taylor, is not your salary due?" Hudson wrote, "I had to swallow two or three times before I could answer. . . . I told him as quietly as I could that it was overdue some little time. How thankful I felt at this moment! God surely had heard my prayer."

The doctor replied, "You know how busy I am. I wish I had thought of it a little sooner, for only this afternoon I sent all the money I had to the bank. Otherwise, I would have paid you at once."

Saturday evening Hudson Taylor, feeling defeated and discouraged, was about to lock the clinic up when the doctor suddenly appeared, rather amused that one of his richest patients had just come by the doctor's home to pay his medical bill.

Hudson too was amused that such a wealthy client would come at 10:00 o'clock at night to pay a bill he could have paid anytime he wanted.

AN ANCIENT MEMORIAL

The doctor then gave Hudson a handful of banknotes and promised to pay him the balance he owned him the next week. What joy Hudson experienced in this answered prayer of faith.[10]

On another occasion, his boss was yet again behind in paying him. Hudson headed home discouraged and confused. He had little money left in his pocket.

While ministering on Sunday evening, he was met by one of the poor men who lived near him in the slum district of London. He begged Hudson to come and see his wife, who had only recently delivered a baby; neither the mother nor the newborn was doing well.

Hudson reluctantly agreed.

He wrote to his sister that he wasn't in the mood to help anybody that night. He was rather frustrated with God at that moment.

When he arrived at the man's apartment, several children were huddled inside the bare, one-room dwelling, which Hudson described as wretched.

A woman was lying on a cot in the corner, and the baby lay in her arms crying. Without any examination, Hudson knew the baby wasn't getting any milk because the woman was malnourished. The entire family was simply hungry. He immediately realized that the Lord wanted him to give this family his remaining money, but his heart refused.

Hudson told the family there was nothing he could do for them. He wrote to his sister:

> I began to tell them . . . they must not be cast down; that though their circumstances were very distressing there was a kind and loving Father in heaven. But something within me cried: "You hypocrite! Telling these unconverted people about a kind and loving Father, and not prepared yourself to trust Him without a half-crown." I was nearly choked [at the thought].[11]

Hudson wrote that he resisted with stubbornness and frustration the obvious desire of God's Spirit for him to completely trust the Lord and give the rest of his money to this family.

He refused.

But he did agree to pray for them. They all knelt down in that little apartment. The battle raged in Taylor's heart and, without any desire or joy, he got up, reached into his pocket, and gave the man all his money. Only then did the joy of the Lord flood his heart. He knew this entire family would soon have food.

When he returned home, he ate his porridge. Before going to bed, he got down on his knees and thanked the Lord that he had been empowered to give everything he had away. Then he reminded the Lord that he was out of money and food.

The next day he received an anonymous package containing a pair of winter gloves. Inside one of the gloves, he found four times the amount of money he had given away the night before.[12]

We would all like to experience this kind of powerful answer to our prayers. But would we be willing to trust God for our income? Would we be willing to trust the Lord to remind our boss to pay us? Would we be willing to give away our last dollar to someone in need?

The truth is that we love the answers of God to acts of faith; we just don't like to go through the agony of acting in faith.

I'm glad Hudson Taylor struggled too—as did Gideon, Samuel, David, and every believer who has ever been honest enough to admit it.

In his later years, Hudson Taylor said, "I used to ask God to help me. Then I asked if I might help Him. I ended up by asking Him to do His work through me." In other words, "I simply cooperate. He does all the rest."

When *that* takes place—that is, when *we* cooperate—*faith* takes place. Our personal weakness does not prohibit our accepting and cooperating with a personal assignment given to us from the hand of God.

What is it that by faith *you* must depend on God alone to fulfill? Are you trusting Him to provide it? Maybe now you are praying as the apostles did when they said to the Lord, "Increase our faith!" (Luke 17:5).

May this be your prayer as well:

> Lord, increase my faith, so that faith will be demonstrated through my weakness as I personally accept—even with hesitation, questions, uncertainty, and with a sense of surprise when something happens—my personal assignment from Your hand . . . my most faithful and gracious Lord.

35b And others were tortured, not accepting their release, so that they might obtain a better resurrection; 36and others experienced mockings and scourgings, yes, also chains and imprisonment. 37They were stoned, they were sawn in two, they were tempted, they were put to death with the sword; they went about in sheepskins, in goatskins, being destitute, afflicted, ill-treated 38(men of whom the world was not worthy), wandering in deserts and mountains and caves and holes in the ground. 39And all these, having gained approval through their faith, did not receive what was promised, 40because God had provided something better for us, so that apart from us they would not be made perfect.

—Hebrews 11:35b–40

CHAPTER TEN

LIVING IN THE SHADOWS

Hebrews 11:35b-40

Born in 1616, John Owen was a leader among Puritan pastors and authors. J. I. Packer described the Puritans as the redwoods in the forest of theology and John Owen as the tallest tree among them.[1] According to Jonathan Edwards, the leader of the Great Awakening in the 1700s, the writings of John Owen were to be valued above any other human author.[2]

John Owen entered Oxford at the age of twelve and graduated with his master's degree at the age of nineteen. He was used by God greatly and became known as the "great doer," because he accomplished so much.

As the chaplain to the king of England and a regular preacher before Parliament, John Owen served in the spotlight. This, however, did not soften or dilute his convictions.

In fact, on one occasion while preaching to the members of Parliament, he rebuked them for fighting against Ireland rather than delivering the gospel to that country and their soldiers. To put that into a contemporary setting, it would be like the chaplain of the United States Senate standing up before all of Congress and rebuking them for fighting a war somewhere rather than delivering the gospel to that country and to the enemy soldiers.

John Owen was a courageous man of faith, preacher, and author. He would fit well among the major characters listed in Hebrews 11 with their stories of courage, victory, progress, and achievement.

But there is another side of John Owen's story that can easily be missed, an element that would not make it into the average church bulletin. He struggled with a lack of consistency and times of spiritual barrenness. Writing to a friend, he confessed:

> I do acknowledge unto you that I have a dry and barren spirit, and I do heartily beg your prayers that the Holy One would, notwithstanding all my sinful provocations, water me from above.[3]

Another important facet of John Owen's life was the suffering he endured. He and his wife, Mary, were married for thirty-one years. They had eleven children, all but one of whom died at a young age. Only one child grew to adulthood—a daughter. But she brought on only more suffering, as she divorced her husband, developed cancer, and moved back into the home of her parents, where she died soon after.

John and Mary Owen walked in the valley of the shadow of death most of their lives. Did that make them people of great faith or little faith?

Does our understanding of faith allow for both, or is great faith observed only on mountaintops? "Is your concept of faith big enough to encompass both the triumphs and tragedies of life?"[4] Hebrews 11 presents both. We find here suffering and victory, sin and grace, failure and progress.

Thus far throughout Hebrews 11, it has been news from the mountaintop. Indeed, if the chapter stopped in the middle of verse 35, readers might get the impression that faith always leads to testimonies of success, glory, and extraordinary achievement. The Christian community today, in fact, is swamped with this lopsided message about faith. Popular preachers and their books, some of which end up on the best-seller lists, promote such falsehoods and misconceptions as the following:

- Faith brings about justice.
- Faithfulness makes the path smooth and blessed.
- Faith creates fearlessness and courage.
- Faithfulness leads to good health and better jobs.
- Faith increases trust, which guarantees less trouble in life.
- Faith makes pain and suffering an exception for the believer.

LIVING IN THE SHADOWS

Believers who absorb ideas like these wake up one day to discover that bad things *do* happen to people who are faithful!

THE SHADOWS OF PERSECUTION

Fortunately, Hebrews 11 does not end in the middle of verse 35. It goes on to include the testimonies of people who lived in the shadows of persecution. They were willing to run the race, even when it looked like they were on the losing team.

Three categories of people are mentioned in this catalog of suffering.

Those Who Were Abused

And others were tortured, not accepting their release, so that they might obtain a better resurrection; and others experienced mockings and scourgings, yes, also chains and imprisonment. (Hebrews 11:35*b*-36)

Others who acted in faith did not see such glorious outcomes as those described in Hebrews 11:32-35*a*. Some, in fact, were tortured because of their faith. It is most likely the author had in view here events from Israel's history during that era between the Old and New Testaments. The literature from that four-hundred-year period tells us that at times faithful believers were severely persecuted for refusing to adopt Greek religion. **Release** and relief could have come had they renounced their faith in the Lord, but they remained faithful, looking forward to something much better than comfort in this life; they looked for a **better resurrection**, when they would be raised to immortal life.

Verse 36 mentions those who **experienced mockings**. This was the case with Nehemiah, who was mocked, scorned, and falsely accused by those who did not want the city of Jerusalem rebuilt (Nehemiah 4–6). The prophet Elisha also was mocked by young men (2 Kings 2:23).

Imagine running a race and no one cheers you on. Instead, everyone jeers, mocks, and ridicules your effort. That is the opposition many Christians endure spiritually around the world today.

This sort of enmity is not new, of course. Think, for instance, of Athanasius, the early church leader who defended the deity of Jesus Christ against the false teachings of some who argued that Christ was simply a human being, glorified only because of his godly life. This was the fourth-century beginning of a heresy that would be repackaged many times over the centuries. It is followed today by the Jehovah's Witnesses and Mormons.

Athanasius was banished from his home in Alexandria five different times, spending a total of seventeen years in exile. He was often alone throughout his fifty years defending Christ's deity and equality with God the Father. He was once told, "Athanasius, the whole world is against you." He replied, "Then Athanasius is against the whole world."[5]

He kept the true gospel—the true faith—even when it meant he would stand alone. Little wonder he was nicknamed "The Saint of Stubbornness."[6]

Hebrews adds that many of the faithful also experienced **scourgings**. Of course, this goes far beyond verbal attacks. The word *scourging* refers to punishment administered by a scourge, a whip with long leather strands. Each strand was weighted by a rock or metal fragment at the tip. This instrument tore into the flesh, bringing the victim to a condition referred to as "half-death."

It is impossible to think of **mockings and scourgings** and not think about the Author and Finisher of our faith—the Lord Jesus—who endured verbal mocking and derision along with such terrible scourging and beatings that he was unrecognizable. Indeed, Christ "gave Himself for us to redeem us from every lawless deed, and to purify for Himself a people for His own possession" (Titus 2:14).

The writer of Hebrews adds one more descriptive phrase of abusive treatment upon the innocent: **yes, also chains and imprisonment.**

The Jewish audience would have thought about Joseph, who was unfairly imprisoned (Genesis 39:20), or the prophet Jeremiah, who was imprisoned for telling the truth to his own king and to his own people (Jeremiah 37:15; 38:6).

These individuals suffered abuse, *not* because they lacked faith, but precisely *because* they demonstrated faith! Their obedience to God made their lives painful, not pleasant.

Those Who Were Martyred

> **They were stoned, they were sawn in two, they were tempted, they were put to death with the sword.** (Hebrews 11:37a)

In verse 37, we read that **they were stoned**. That is, rocks were thrown at them at close range in order to kill them. Sophisticated weapons, swords, or a hangman's noose were not needed, just rocks.

Naboth was falsely accused by King Ahab and his wife Jezebel and then stoned to death (1 Kings 21:1-14). According to Jewish tradition, Jeremiah the prophet was eventually executed by stoning. And in the New Testament era Stephen was stoned to death after his sermon declaring the deity and glory of Jesus Christ (Acts 7:58-59).

The writer adds that some **were sawn in two**. Jewish tradition has held for centuries that King Manasseh hunted down the prophet Isaiah because he dared to deliver the word of God's judgment against Judah. At first, Isaiah escaped by hiding in a hollow tree, but he was eventually discovered, and the king ordered the tree sawed in half with Isaiah inside it.[7]

The writer goes on to add that **they were tempted**. More than likely, this is a reference to those tempted to recant their faith in order to save their lives. The ones who did not recant **were put to death by the sword**.

In the vicinity of the Italian capital, Rome, there are sixty catacombs covering more than six hundred miles of tunnels and galleries underground. These tunnels, or catacombs, are about eight feet high and from three to five feet wide, with rows of long recessed areas built off to the side. The deceased were placed in these recesses, which were then closed or covered by a marble slab or large tiles. When Christian graves in the catacombs were later opened and explored, many skeletal remains revealed terrible suffering from Roman persecution. Heads were severed from bodies, ribs and shoulder blades were broken, and bones were blackened from fire.[8]

The *St. Petersburg Times* covered the story of a Ukrainian man who was mauled by a lioness at the Kyiv Zoo. He encountered the animal on purpose, believing that God would protect him. The man lowered himself by a rope into a concrete enclosure that held four lions. Then he walked toward them, shouting, "God will save me if He exists." One lioness knocked him to the ground, severing his carotid artery as a huge crowd helplessly watched from above.[9]

Was his faith not great enough? Faith, of course, is not an issue in this situation. No one should test God like that! Yet many do. There are believers who handle rattlesnakes in their worship services, convinced that their faith will keep them alive if they are bitten. Others refuse medication, believing that to do so would be an insult to their faith in a true and living God.

Most Christians would never do such things. Still, millions are confronted with a crisis of faith in God because He did not rescue them from danger, disability, difficulty, or perhaps the death of a loved one. They act in faith, trust the Lord, and do everything they reasonably can to avoid tragedy, but they still suffer. They might not say it out loud, but their hearts cry, "If God exists, why did He not save me from this?" If you have felt that way, you are not alone.

When hardship comes, the human heart naturally wonders where God went. Like Job, we ask where God has gone and demand an audience with our Creator.

God hasn't gone anywhere. Learn that from Hebrews 11—the entire chapter. It's obvious God is present in the first part of the chapter, as walls tumble, seas part, and the dead are raised to life. He is in this last part of the chapter as well. The only difference is that He remains in the shadows where we can't sense His power or presence.

James Russell Lowell penned it so well when he wrote:

> *Truth forever on the scaffold,*
> *Wrong forever on the throne—*
> *Yet that scaffold sways the future, and,*
> *behind the dim unknown,*
> *Standeth God within the shadow,*
> *keeping watch above his own.*[10]

We know God is with us when we live in the sunshine. But He is also with us when we live in the shadows. He walks with His beloved always, even through the valley of the shadow of death.

Those Who Were Ignored and Abandoned

They went about in sheepskins, in goatskins, being destitute, afflicted, ill-treated (men of whom the world was not worthy), wandering in deserts and mountains and caves and holes in the ground. (Hebrews 11:37*b*-38)

Sheepskins and goatskins indicate that these people of faith had no other material for clothing—no silk, cotton, or linen. The clothes they wore were made of the most primitive material reserved for the poor: dried leather skins of sheep and goats.

The text describes them further as **destitute, afflicted, ill-treated**. These are three present-tense passive participles in the Greek language. This indicates they were *constantly* **destitute**—they did not know where their next drink of water or bite of food would come from; they were *constantly* **afflicted**—they lived under great stress and pressure as they tried to survive; and they were *constantly* **ill-treated**—they were tormented or oppressed.[11]

These heroes of the faith were driven from their homes. They were not only abandoned but also disowned. We read in verse 38 that they lived **wandering in deserts and mountains and caves and holes in the ground**. After being reduced to the most basic forms of living, they found refuge in caves and other crude dwellings dug into the ground.

- David hid out in the wilderness from King Saul (1 Samuel 22).
- Obadiah fed prophets who were hiding out in a cave (1 Kings 18:3-4).
- Elijah ran for his life and hid in a cave from Jezebel's assassins (1 Kings 19:9).
- Christians hid in the catacombs of Rome during years of persecution.[12]

According to the standards of this world, *they* were losers. But according to God's standards, they were people **of whom the world was not worthy**. They were disowned by their own people but adopted by their heavenly Father! They were ignored by their world but loved by their Savior! There was no home for them on earth but a magnificent home awaited them in heaven!

The description **of whom the world was not worthy** reminds us that outward appearances do not always reflect reality. The stories of these people of faith did not *end* with loss. They actually won. Similarly, our story does not end with difficulties and trials . . . the believer wins!

While God calls some to win by living, others He calls to win by dying.[13] Some are called to win through triumph; others are called to win through tragedy. Paul put it this way: "To live is Christ and to die is gain" (Philippians 1:21).

Martyred missionaries like Nate Saint and Jim Elliot were not losers but winners. The cause of Christ won with their martyrdoms. The cause of Christ is also winning today in China, Vietnam, North Africa, Pakistan, and North Korea.

Was God losing when His Son stood before Pilate and then hung on a cross? The answer depends on where you stop the story. Likewise, Hebrews 11 teaches us the story is not over yet.

Who was winning—Hitler or Corrie ten Boom? Corrie ten Boom entered the concentration camp at Ravensbruck along with thousands of women. As a believer incarcerated for aiding Jews escaping from the Nazi death camps, Corrie was now among them. She was able to smuggle a small Bible into the camp. She explained its importance:

> From morning until lights-out, whenever we were not in ranks for roll call, our Bible was the center of an ever-widening circle of help and hope. Like waifs clustered around a blazing fire, we gathered about it, holding out our hearts to its warmth and light.[14]

On December 31, 1944, "by a clerical error of man and a miracle of God," as Corrie worded it, she was released. Already fifty-two years old, she would spend the rest of her single life traveling and testifying powerfully "that there is no pit so deep that He [God] is not deeper still."[15]

Who won?

THE SHADOWS OF PROMISE

And all these, having gained approval through their faith, did not receive what was promised, because God had

provided something better for us, so that apart from us they would not be made perfect. (Hebrews 11:39-40)

Although these heroes of the faith were overcomers, their story was not completed, or **made perfect**, without **us** New Testament believers. That is, their salvation by faith is bound up with ours. God's plan leaves out no one who trusts in Him, whether before Christ's coming or after.

The Old Testament saints looked forward to promises still unfulfilled in their time—particularly, those associated with the promised Messiah, whose death on the cross would complete, or perfect, their redemption.

Our perspective as New Testament believers is superior to theirs since we have God's completed revelation in His Word. The historical facts of Christ's coming, dying, and rising from the dead have been revealed to us in detail. We have both the Old and the New Testament available to us.

We today live in the full disclosure of the sunlight of God's Word; they lived in the shadows of promises yet to be fulfilled. They did not have Matthew through Revelation. They had no written description of the Father's House, the tree of life, and the glorious new heaven and earth. They knew nothing of Christ's judgment seat, where they will be rewarded for their labor of love and their acts of faith, and nothing of that final statement of satisfaction, when Jesus Christ said, "It is finished!" They knew little or nothing of the Holy Spirit—our ever-present Counselor and Comforter. But they acted in obedience to the revelation God gave them, and what a testimony to their faith that is!

If they were able to trust God when they had so little revelation from Him, what are we doing for God with a completed revelation?

John Calvin wrote on this text: "A tiny spark of light led them to heaven, but now that the Sun of righteousness shines on us what excuse shall we offer if we still cling to the earth?"[16]

They persevered in faith, and they did not know half what we know today; however, their perseverance and trust encourage us to demonstrate lives of faith in God.

One author wrote this:

> Those ancient saints form our spiritual family tree. Without them, we have no roots. Without us, they have no branches. They are "made perfect," or *completed*, as the life-giving sap

of their lives flows through our spiritual leaves and flowers to fill the earth with the fragrance of faith.[17]

A hundred years ago a hymn writer fashioned the perfect words for our hearts today. I sang those words with my extended family several years ago as we gathered in the home of my younger brother who was dying of brain cancer. His tumor had spread, and his pain increased. The recent MRI showed the white film of cancer in both hemispheres. Despite all that, he remained lucid, still fighting, and still very funny. Above all that, he was still trusting, singing, and verbalizing that God is worth following in the sunshine and in the shadows.

We had formed a huge circle to pray when he said, "Let's sing." And he began to lead us in singing:

> *Great is thy faithfulness, Oh God my Father,*
> *There is no shadow of turning with Thee.*
> *Thou changest not, Thy compassions they fail not;*
> *As Thou has been Thou forever wilt be.*
>
> *Great is Thy faithfulness! Great is Thy faithfulness!*
> *Morning by morning new mercies I see;*
> *All I have needed Thy hand hath provided—*
> *Great is thy faithfulness, Lord unto me!*[18]

This was true for all the saints in Hebrews 11 who experienced the sunshine, and for all those who suffered in the shadows. God was there all along. Faith means running the race, even when it looks like you're losing—and you are *not*!

This race of faith will end when, among other things, our racing is exchanged for reigning—reigning with our coming, conquering King.

So, don't stop now . . . it doesn't end here.

ENDNOTES

CHAPTER ONE

1. *Mosby's Pocket Dictionary of Medicine, Nursing and Health Professions*, Sixth Edition (Mosby Elsevier, 2010), s.v. "pasteurization," "pasteurized milk," "Louis Pasteur."
2. Alan C. Jackson, ed. *Rabies: Scientific Basis of the Disease and Its Management*, Third Edition (Academic Press, 2013), 3-7.
3. Axel Munthe, *The Story of San Michele* (E. P. Dutton & Co., Inc., 1930), 66.
4. For a long list that Carver himself compiled of products he developed from peanuts and sweet potatoes, see "Appendix 2" in Christina Vella, *George Washington Carver: A Life* (Louisiana State University Press, 2015).
5. Jill Morgan, *A Man of the Word: Life of G. Campbell Morgan* (Wipf & Stock, 2010), 13.
6. Edgar Andrews, *A Glorious High Throne* (Evangelical Press, 2003), 342.
7. Kenneth S. Wuest, *Hebrews in the Greek New Testament* (Eerdmans, 1947), 193.
8. Michael Horton, *The Gospel-Driven Life* (Baker Books, 2009), 123.
9. John MacArthur, Jr., *The Power of Faith Study Guide* (Word of Grace Communications, 1987), 9.
10. Peter T. O'Brien, *The Letter to the Hebrews* (Eerdmans, 2010), 399.
11. Thomas Manton, *Sermons on Hebrews 11* (The Banner of Truth Trust, 2000), 24.
12. Adapted from Bruce B. Barton, Dave Veerman, and Linda K. Taylor, *Life Application Bible Commentary: Hebrews* (The Livingstone Corporation, 1997), 176.
13. Thomas D. Lea, *Holman New Testament Commentary: Hebrews & James* (Broadman and Holman, 1999), 200.
14. G. Campbell Morgan, *The Triumphs of Faith: Expositions of Hebrews 11* (Baker Book House, 1980), 21.
15. William White Jr., "Legion," in *The Zondervan Pictorial Encyclopedia of the Bible*, Volume 3, edited by Merrill Tenney (Zondervan, 1975), 907-8.

CHAPTER TWO

1. Adapted from Darrell W. Johnson, *The Glory of Preaching: Participating in God's Transformation of the World* (InterVarsity, 2009), 67.
2. Quoted by Nancy R. Pearcey, "The Birds and the Bees. Pop Culture's Evolutionary Message: I'm an Animal, You're an Animal, Wouldn't You Like to Be an Animal Too?" *World Magazine* (April 2000), 21.
3. Sean Carroll, *The Big Picture on the Origins of Life, Meaning and the Universe Itself* (Oneworld Publications, 2016), 215-21.

[4] Charles Darwin (1809–82), *On Evolution: The Development of the Theory of Natural Selection*, edited by Thomas F. Glick and David Kohn (Hackett Publishing Company, 1996), 58, 66, 92, 214.

[5] Darwin Correspondence Project, "To J. D. Hooker 1 February [1871]," University of Cambridge, www.darwinproject.ac.uk (accessed January 15, 2019).

[6] George Wald, "The Origin of Life," *Scientific American*, Vol. 191, Issue 2 (August 1954), 46.

[7] Ibid., 47-48.

[8] Ibid., 48.

[9] Francis Darwin, ed., *The Life and Letters of Charles Darwin, including An Autobiographical Chapter*, Vol. 2 (John Murray, Albemarle Street, 1887), 353-54.

[10] Kenneth S. Wuest, *Hebrews in the Greek New Testament* (Eerdmans, 1969), 195.

[11] R. Kent Hughes, *Hebrews: An Anchor for the Soul* (Crossway, 2015), 292-93.

[12] Fritz Rienecker and Cleon Rogers, *Linguistic Key to the Greek New Testament* (Zondervan, 1976), 706.

[13] John MacArthur Jr., *The Battle for the Beginning* (W Publishing Group, 2001), 55.

[14] Ibid.

[15] Charles Colson and Nancy Pearcey, *How Now Shall We Live?* (Tyndale House, 1999), 98.

[16] See the description in Wayne Grudem, *Systematic Theology: An Introduction to Biblical Doctrine* (Zondervan, 1994), 276-79.

[17] J. P. Moreland et. al., eds., *Theistic Evolution: A Scientific, Philosophical, and Theological Critique* (Crossway, 2017).

[18] R. Kent Hughes, *Genesis: Beginning and Blessing* (Crossway, 2004), 19.

[19] Kendrick Frazier, "Competence and Controversy," *Skeptical Inquirer*, Volume 8 (1983), 2-5.

[20] John Patterson, "Do Scientists and Educators Discriminate Unfairly Against Creationists?" *Journal of the National Center for Science Education* (1984), 19.

[21] Carl Sagan, *Pale Blue Dot: A Vision of the Human Future in Space* (Random House, 1994), 7.

[22] Colson and Pearcey, 97.

[23] Christopher Catherwood, *Five Evangelical Leaders* (Christian Focus:, 1994), 135-36; cited in Douglas F. Kelly, *Creation and Change: Genesis 1.1–2.4 in the Light of Changing Scientific Paradigms* (Christian Focus, 2015), 23-244.

CHAPTER THREE

[1] Joel Osteen, *I Declare: 31 Promises to Speak over Your Life* (FaithWords, 2013), 1.

[2] Michele Straubel, "The Art of Maple Sugaring Compared to the Discipleship Process," Sermon Illustrations, preachingtoday.com.

[3] John MacArthur, *The MacArthur New Testament Commentary: Hebrews* (Moody, 1983), 296.

[4] Thomas Manton, *By Faith: Sermons on Hebrews 11* (The Banner of Truth Trust, 2000), 115.

[5] R. Kent Hughes, *Hebrews: An Anchor for the Soul* (Crossway, 2015), 296.

[6] Manton, 122.

[7] MacArthur, 299.

[8] Kenneth S. Wuest, *Hebrews in the Greek New Testament* (Eerdmans, 1969), 197.

[9] Horatius Bonar, "Not What These Hands Have Done."

[10] Lidie H. Edmunds, "My Faith Has Found A Resting Place."

CHAPTER FOUR

[1] Elmer B. Smick, "Methuselah," in *The Zondervan Pictorial Encyclopedia of the Bible*, Volume 4, edited by Merrill Tenney (Zondervan, 1975), 212; Francis Brown, S. R. Driver, and Charles A. Briggs, *A Hebrew and English Lexicon of the Old Testament* (Clarendon, 1978), 607.

[2] Stelman Smith and Judson Cornwall, *The Exhaustive Dictionary of Bible Names* (Bridge-Logos, 1998), 128. See also James Montgomery Boice, *Genesis: An Expositional Commentary*, Volume 1 (Zondervan, 1982), 232.

[3] Boice, 235.

[4] R. Kent Hughes, *Genesis: Beginning and Blessing* (Crossway, 2004), 120.

[5] Adapted from R. Kent Hughes, *Hebrews: An Anchor for the Soul* (Crossway, 2015), 305-6.

[6] Thomas Manton, *By Faith: Sermons on Hebrews 11* (The Banner of Truth Trust, 2000), 20-21.

[7] G. Ch. Aalders, *Genesis*, Volume 1 (Zondervan, 1981), 141.

[8] Gerhard Friedrich, ed., *Theological Dictionary of the New Testament*, Volume 8 (Eerdmans, 1964), 161.

[9] Warren W. Wiersbe, *Run with the Winners: Developing a Championship Lifestyle from Hebrews 11* (Kregel, 1995), 43.

[10] Boice, 231.

[11] Adapted from G. Campbell Morgan, *The Triumphs of Faith: Expositions of Hebrews 11* (Baker Book House, 1980), 66.

CHAPTER FIVE

[1] John Bunyan, *The Pilgrim's Progress: From This World to That Which Is to Come* (Logos Research Systems, Inc.).

[2] Adapted from Henry Morris, *The Genesis Record* (Baker, 1976), 174.

[3] Charles R. Swindoll, *The Practical Life of Faith: A Study of Hebrews 11–13* (Insight for Living, 1989), 12.

[4] James Montgomery Boice, *Genesis*, Volume 1 (Zondervan, 1982), 189.

[5] R. Kent Hughes, *Hebrews: An Anchor for the Soul* (Crossway, 2015), 316.

[6] Bruce B. Barton, Dave Veerman, and Linda K. Taylor, *Life Application Bible Commentary: Hebrews* (The Livingstone Corporation, 1997), 181.

[7] John MacArthur Jr., *The MacArthur New Testament Commentary: Hebrews* (Moody, 1983), 320.

[8] John C. Whitcomb, *The World That Perished*, second edition (Baker, 1988), 25.

[9] Ibid.

[10] Richard D. Phillips, *Hebrews* (P&R Publishing, 2006), 433.

[11] William Barclay, *The Letter to the Hebrews* (Westminster John Knox Press, 1976), 142.

[12] Ibid.

[13] *The History of Little Goody Two-Shoes* (Project Gutenberg eBook reprint), gutenberg.org.

[14] A. W. Tozer, *The Root of the Righteous* (Moody, 1989), 189.

[15] MacArthur, 319.

[16] Morris, 182.

[17] Phillips, 434

[18] James Montgomery Boice, *Genesis*, Volume 1 (Zondervan, 1982), 283-84.

[19] Ken Ham, *Did Adam Have A Bellybutton? And Other Tough Questions about the Bible* (Master Books, 2009), 39.

[20] Whitcomb, 69-70.

[21] Ibid., 69.

[22] Ken Ham, *The Great Dinosaur Mystery Solved: A Biblical View of These Amazing Creatures* (Master Books, 2000), 18.

[23] Don Batten, et. al., *The Answers Book* (Master Books, 1990), 180.

[24] Whitcomb, 26.

[25] Ibid., 34.

CHAPTER SIX

[1] Russell Kelso Carter, "Standing on the Promises."

[2] R. Kent Hughes, *Hebrews: An Anchor for the Soul* (Crossway, 2015), 323.

[3] G. Campbell Morgan, *The Triumphs of Faith: Expositions of Hebrews 11* (Baker, 1980), 142.

[4] Ibid., 78.

[5] Hughes, 324.

[6] Adapted from ibid., 325.

[7] John MacArthur, *The MacArthur New Testament Commentary: Hebrews* (Moody, 1983), 330.

[8] Bruce B. Barton, Dave Veerman, and Linda K. Taylor, *Life Application Bible Commentary: Hebrews* (The Livingstone Corporation, 1997), 182.

[9] Adapted from Charles R. Swindoll, *The Practical Life of Faith: A Study of Hebrews 11* (Insight for Living, 1989), 18.

[10] Donald Grey Barnhouse, *Romans*, Volume 2 (Eerdmans, 1982), 312.

[11] Howard Taylor, *Hudson Taylor and the China Inland Mission* (OMF International, 1996), 31.

[12] William Barclay, *The Letter to the Hebrews* (Westminster John Knox Press, 1976), 148.

[13] David E. Aune, *The Westminster Dictionary of New Testament and Early Christian Literature and Rhetoric* (Westminster John Knox Press, 2003), 137.

[14] See Leah MarieAnn Klett, "Legendary Songwriter Don Moen Reveals Heartbreaking Story Behind "God Will Make a Way," *Christian Examiner*, October 24, 2018, christianexaminer.com.

[15] Don Moen, "God Will Make a Way," copyright © 1990 Integrity's Hosanna! Music (ASCAP) (adm. at CapitolCMGPublishing.com). All rights reserved. Used by permission.

CHAPTER SEVEN

[1] Orrin Woodward, *Resolved: 13 Resolutions for LIFE* (New Century Publishing, 2011), 269.

[2] Ibid., 117.

[3] Charles R. Swindoll, *Moses: A Man of Selfless Dedication* (Thomas Nelson, 1999), 23.

[4] Bernard L. Ramm, *God's Way Out* (Regal Books, 1987), 18.

[5] Swindoll, 26.

[6] Ramm, 18.

⁷ Charles R. Swindoll, *The Practical Life of Faith: A Study of Hebrews 11–13* (Insight for Living, 1989), 37.

⁸ Stanley Outlaw, *The Book of Hebrews* (Randall House, 2005), 297.

⁹ G. Campbell Morgan, *The Triumphs of Faith: Expositions of Hebrews 11* (Baker Book House, 1980), 125.

¹⁰ R. Kent Hughes, *Hebrews: An Anchor for the Soul* (Crossway, 2015), 348.

¹¹ Ibid., 343.

¹² Jesse Clement, *The Life of Rev. Adoniram Judson* (University of Michigan Library reprint), 25.

CHAPTER EIGHT

¹ Michael P. Green, ed., *1500 Illustrations for Biblical Preaching* (Baker, 1989), 145.

² C. F. Keil and F. Delitzsch, *Commentary on the Old Testament*, Volume 1 (Eerdmans, 1991), 53.

³ Arthur W. Pink, *An Exposition of Hebrews*, Volume 2 (Baker, 1963), 834.

⁴ John Phillips, *Exploring Hebrews* (Loizeaux Brothers, 1988), 164.

⁵ Pink, *Hebrews*, 836.

⁶ Dr. and Mrs. Howard Taylor, *Hudson Taylor and the China Inland Mission: Volume 2* (OMF International, 1996), 276.

⁷ Jesse Clement, *The Life of Rev. Adoniram Judson* (University of Michigan Library reprint), 250.

⁸ G. Campbell Morgan, *The Triumphs of Faith: Expositions of Hebrews 11* (Baker, 1980), 149.

⁹ W. H. Griffith Thomas, *Hebrews: A Devotional Commentary* (Eerdmans, 1982), 154.

¹⁰ Taylor, 265.

CHAPTER NINE

¹ Charles R. Swindoll, *The Practical Life of Faith: A Study of Hebrews 11–13* (Insight for Living, 1989), 53. See also Vietnam Veterans Memorial Fund, vvmf.org.

² "Gettysburg Address," Microsoft® Encarta. Funk & Wagnall's, 1994.

³ Arthur W. Pink, *An Exposition of Hebrews*, Volume 2 (Baker, 1963), 848.

⁴ Ibid., 855.

⁵ These stories are recounted in Philip Mason, *Niagara and the Daredevils* (Niagara Daredevil Gallery, 1969).

⁶ R. Kent Hughes, *Hebrews: An Anchor for the Soul* (Crossway, 2015), 376.

[7] Edgar Andrews, *A Glorious High Throne* (Evangelical Press, 2003), 396.

[8] John Phillips, *Exploring Hebrews* (Loizeaux Brothers, 1988), 169.

[9] See Stephen Davey, *Legacies of Light* (Charity House, 2019), 92-94.

[10] Dr. and Mrs. Howard Taylor, *Hudson Taylor in Early Years: The Growth of a Soul* (OMF International, 1996), 67.

[11] Ibid., 136-37.

[12] Ibid., 135.

CHAPTER TEN

[1] Cited by John Piper in *Contending for Our All: Defending Truth and Treasuring Christ in the Lives of Athanasius, John Owen, and J. Gresham Machen* (Crossway, 2006), 79.

[2] Ibid., 82.

[3] Ibid., 109.

[4] George H. Guthrie, "Hebrews" in *Zondervan Illustrated Bible Backgrounds Commentary*, ed. Clinton E. Arnold, Vol. 4 (Zondervan, 2002), 73.

[5] John MacArthur Jr., *Twelve Unlikely Heroes* (Thomas Nelson, 2012), 1.

[6] Ibid., 2.

[7] Bruce B. Barton, Dave Veerman, and Linda K. Taylor, *Life Application Bible Commentary: Hebrews* (The Livingstone Corporation, 1997), 200.

[8] Charles R. Swindoll, *The Practical Life of Faith: A Study of Hebrews 11–13* (Insight for Living, 1989), 54.

[9] "Lion Kills Man in Kiev," *St. Petersburg Times*, June 5, 2006.

[10] James Russell Lowell, "The Present Crisis."

[11] Kenneth S. Wuest, *Hebrews in the Greek New Testament* (Eerdmans, 1969), 210.

[12] W. Stanley Outlaw, *Hebrews* (Randall House Publications, 2005), 313.

[13] James Montgomery Boice, *Daniel* (Baker, 1989), 72.

[14] Lawrence Kimbrough, *Words to Die For* (Broadman and Holman, 2002), 167-68.

[15] Ibid., 168-69.

[16] Richard D. Phillips, *Hebrews* (P&R Publishing, 2006), 526.

[17] Swindoll, 55.

[18] Thomas O. Chisolm, "Great Is Thy Faithfulness."

SCRIPTURE INDEX

Reference	Page
Genesis 1–5	33
Genesis 1:11	21
Genesis 1:14-18	21
Genesis 2:16-17	30
Genesis 3	30
Genesis 3:15	31
Genesis 3:21	31
Genesis 3:24	34
Genesis 4	33/34/42
Genesis 4:1	31
Genesis 4:3-4*a*	32
Genesis 4:4b-5*a*	36
Genesis 4:4b-5	32
Genesis 4:19	55
Genesis 4:22	56
Genesis 4:23	42/56
Genesis 4:24	42
Genesis 5	42/44/45
Genesis 5:5	33
Genesis 5:18-24	41
Genesis 5:21	43
Genesis 5:22	46
Genesis 5:24	50
Genesis 6	57/58
Genesis 6–9	34/63
Genesis 6:1	56
Genesis 6:3	58
Genesis 6:4	56
Genesis 6:5	55/56/60
Genesis 6:8	63

Reference	Page
Genesis 6:9	56
Genesis 6:12	56
Genesis 6:13-14	58
Genesis 6:14	63/72
Genesis 6:14-22	58
Genesis 6:17	58
Genesis 7	57/67/71
Genesis 7:11	69
Genesis 7:16	64
Genesis 7:17-22	68
Genesis 7:24–8:3	69
Genesis 8:13-14	69
Genesis 8:17	72
Genesis 9:8-17	68
Genesis 9:20	58
Genesis 9:28-29	44
Genesis 12	77
Genesis 39:20	126
Exodus 1:15-22	89
Exodus 2	90
Exodus 2:3	90
Exodus 2:10	91
Exodus 2:14*b*-15	94
Exodus 12	95
Exodus 14:11-12	100
Exodus 14:13-14	101
Exodus 14:21	101
Exodus 14:22	101
Exodus 15:8	101
Exodus 25:17-22	35

Reference	Page
Exodus 26	35
Leviticus 9:24	37
Leviticus 16	35
Numbers 22:28	72
Numbers 24:21	72
Deuteronomy 1:28	102
Deuteronomy 22:6	72
Joshua 2:1	105
Joshua 2:9	105
Joshua 2:10	104
Joshua 2:11	105
Joshua 6:1-6	103
Judges 4–5	112
Judges 6–8	111
Judges 6:21	37
Judges 11	113
Judges 13–16	112
1 Samuel 17	113
1 Samuel 18	116
1 Samuel 22	129
1 Kings 6:23-28	35
1 Kings 17:6	72
1 Kings 17:17-24	116
1 Kings 18:3-4	129
1 Kings 18:38	37
1 Kings 19:9	129
1 Kings 21:1-14	127
2 Kings 2:23	125
2 Kings 4:18-37	116
2 Kings 6	14

Reference	Page
2 Kings 6:15	14
2 Kings 6:16	14
2 Kings 6:17	14
1 Chronicles 21:26	37
2 Chronicles 7:1	37
Nehemiah 4–6	125
Psalm 33:6	23
Psalm 33:8-12	23
Psalm 43:3	49
Psalm 73:24	49
Psalm 84:3	72
Psalm 104	69
Isaiah 10:14	72
Isaiah 54:9	65
Jeremiah 37:15	126
Jeremiah 38:6	126
Jeremiah 39	116
Ezekiel 14:14	65
Ezekiel 14:20	65
Daniel 6:21-22	72
Jonah 1:17	72
Jonah 2:10	72
Matthew 1:5-6	106
Matthew 17:27	72
Matthew 24:37-39	65/68
Matthew 26:52-53	15
Luke 3:36	65
Luke 17:5	120
Luke 17:28	56
Luke 22:42	38

Reference	Page
John 1:1	24
John 1:12	24
John 1:14	24
John 6:37	64
John 10:9	64
John 14	26
John 14:6	64
John 15:5	116
John 19:30	36
Acts 7:2	76
Acts 7:22	91
Acts 7:58-59	127
Acts 17	26
Romans 8:23	12
Romans 15:4	8
1 Corinthians 10:11	8
1 Corinthians 15:52	50
2 Corinthians 4:16-18	93
2 Corinthians 5:20	12
Ephesians 2:8-9	63
Ephesians 6:16	116
Philippians 1:21	130
Colossians 3:12-25	12
1 Thessalonians 1:10	12
1 Thessalonians 4:13-18	50
1 Thessalonians 4:16-17	64
Titus 2:13	49
Titus 2:14	126
Hebrews 6:12	8/15
Hebrews 10	9

Reference	Page
Hebrews 10:35	9
Hebrews 11	10/15/29/47/48/55/61/81/88/99/105/117/124/12
Hebrews 11:1	9
Hebrews 11:1a	10
Hebrews 11:1b	13
Hebrews 11:1-2	6
Hebrews 11:2	15
Hebrews 11:3	16/20/22/23/27
Hebrews 11:4	28/33/37
Hebrews 11:4a	30
Hebrews 11:4b	36
Hebrews 11:4c	38
Hebrews 11:5	49
Hebrews 11:5-6	40/41
Hebrews 11:6	47
Hebrews 11:7	52/54/55/57
Hebrews 11:8	77
Hebrews 11:8-10	76
Hebrews 11:8-22	74
Hebrews 11:9	77
Hebrews 11:10	77
Hebrews 11:11-12	78
Hebrews 11:12	80/82
Hebrews 11:13	81
Hebrews 11:13-16	80
Hebrews 11:16	81
Hebrews 11:17-19	82
Hebrews 11:19	83

Reference	Page
Hebrews 11:20	81
Hebrews 11:20-22	80
Hebrews 11:21	81
Hebrews 11:22	81
Hebrews 11:23	88
Hebrews 11:23-28	86
Hebrews 11:24	88/92
Hebrews 11:24-26	91
Hebrews 11:25	92
Hebrews 11:26	93
Hebrews 11:27	88/93/94
Hebrews 11:28	88/95
Hebrews 11:29	100/102
Hebrews 11:29-31	98
Hebrews 11:30	102
Hebrews 11:31	104/105
Hebrews 11:32	110/111
Hebrews 11:32-35*a*	108/125
Hebrews 11:33	110
Hebrews 11:33-35*a*	115
Hebrews 11:35	110/124/125
Hebrews 11:35*b*-36	125
Hebrews 11:35*b*-40	122
Hebrews 11:36	125
Hebrews 11:37	127
Hebrews 11:37*a*	127
Hebrews 11:37*b*-38	129
Hebrews 11:38	129
Hebrews 11:39-40	131
Hebrews 12	9

Reference	Page
Hebrews 12:1	9
Hebrews 12:22	77
Hebrews 13:7	15
James 2:25	105
1 Peter 3:6	78
1 Peter 3:18-20	56
1 Peter 5:8	115
2 Peter 2:5	56/59/65
2 Peter 3:5-7	68
2 Peter 3:10-13	61
Jude 11	34
Jude 14	43
Jude 14*a*	42
Jude 14-15	41/43
Revelation 4–19	64
Revelation 21:1	61/64

Made in the USA
Columbia, SC
03 April 2025

8edc9f30-2724-4aa3-8fcf-473ffef1151eR01